Social Data Analytics
Collaboration for the Enterprise

Social Data Analytics
Collaboration for the Enterprise

Krish Krishnan

Shawn P. Rogers

AMSTERDAM • BOSTON • HEIDELBERG • LONDON
NEW YORK • OXFORD • PARIS • SAN DIEGO
SAN FRANCISCO • SINGAPORE • SYDNEY • TOKYO
Morgan Kaufmann is an Imprint of Elsevier

Acquiring Editor: Steve Elliot
Editorial Project Manager: Kaitlin Herbert
Project Manager: Priya Kumaraguruparan
Designer: Matthew Limbert

Morgan Kaufmann is an imprint of Elsevier
225 Wyman Street, Waltham, MA 02451, USA

British Library Cataloguing-in-Publication Data
A catalogue record for this book is available from the British Library

Library of Congress Cataloging-in-Publication Data
A catalog record for this book is available from the Library of Congress

ISBN: 978-0-12-397186-9

For information on all Morgan Kaufmann publications
visit our website at http://store.elsevier.com/

Working together
to grow libraries in
developing countries

www.elsevier.com • www.bookaid.org

Dedication

This book is dedicated to

My wife Poornima and our sons Anirrudh and Akash. You guys are my pillar of support in this endless dream to share the knowledge.

My friends Todd Nash, Peter Geovanes, Shankar Radhakrishnan and Nagaphani Nysavajulla, four best buddies of mine who have lived this dream in different projects we have done so far.

Krish Krishnan

A special thank you to Dawn, Amanda and Jack for all of your support and love.

Shawn P. Rogers

Contents

List of figures

Acknowledgments

This book would not have been possible without the support of many people, and I would like to acknowledge them and thank them for all their help. First and foremost, I would like to thank my ever-supportive family of my wife and my two sons, who sacrificed many weekends, holidays, and school and social events (where I was absent) to provide me the quality time needed to think in developing the content of this book. Without your help and support, I would have never been able to dream and write this book.

My coauthor and the guy whose dream it was to write this book, he teaches this subject at many conferences and events—Shawn Rogers. You have been very supportive in the shaping of the book and your immense giving of time and runway for me to author the book, while sharing your ideas in several weekend phone calls and conference meetings between the busy schedules we share.

A very warm, big, and special thanks to my dear friend and supporter Claudia Imhoff. Without your guidance, there were times where I might have said it is time to reevaluate and discontinue the project. Thanks Claudia for the kind words and encouragement.

No book can be written based on theories alone—here is where many industry veterans came to help in the form of vendor support. I would like to thank all of you for the numerous case studies and information you shared in your own internal and customer journeys on this subject.

There are several friends who supported me in this journey with words of encouragement who I would like to mention and thank: Paul Kautza, Laura Reeves, Philip Russom, Dave Stodder, Dave Wells, Jill Dyche, Mark Madsen, John Myers, William McKinght, and John Lucas.

Last, but not the least, my thanks to my editors Steve Elliot and Kaitlin Herbert for the tireless hours of discussions, follow-through, and weekends of time we spent on this project to bring it to fruition. Thanks as well to the entire team at Morgan Kauffman for all the help, guidance, and support in this process—without you, none of this would have been possible.

Thanks!

Preface

Social analytics in the enterprise? Is this hype or reality? Are we talking of making the enterprise more social media aware or are we talking about creating a social media platform? A platform that the enterprise will use to consume information for evolving and maturing opportunities and insights that otherwise might not have been identified? Why discuss social media analytics, and what is so different or cool about it? We have heard these questions over and again in our daily work as analysts, speakers, faculty, and management consultants. This book has evolved from our five years of research and discussions on this very topic.

The content as presented here is not a technical treatise nor is it a management strategy book replete with stories and discussion points; rather, it is a combination of both and written to be thought provoking and provide information that can be applicable to any company in any field. As you finish each chapter, you'll be able to create new and improved business strategies that will immediately improve internal collaboration and information usage.

Social media as an industry has evolved over the last decade from simple web forums or web pages of information sharing to a well-oiled search and exploratory taxonomy with multiple services and organizations such as Twitter, Facebook, Instagram, Skype, Whatsapp and Pintrest. Thus, creating a well-rounded community or communities around different subjects of interest, and in the process establishing a virtual world where connectivity and collaboration happens in an instant. This evolution has created a community where information gathered from consumers can be leveraged in the form of advertising and marketing that leads to tangible sales. The backbone of these new information-gathering techniques are crowd-sourcing and implementation of algorithms such as recommendation engines along with statistical clusters and common dimensionality for semantic identification, classification, clustering, homograph resolution, contextualization, and visualization. The evolving and changing social media universe and as a result the analytic output is being embraced by organizations in order to foster a customer-centric transformation. We have included several case studies throughout the book discussing the journey taken by companies that are now leaders in the social media analytics space.

Our goal in presenting this material is to enable you to think strategically about how to create and leverage social media analytics inside your enterprise. The outcome of establishing a program such as this will bring an increased internal focus on collaboration and information sharing to what had been disparate groups. In this evolved organization, sales, marketing, finance, supply chain, and inventory management will all work together from one data platform where they share information and create insights and visibility. A brief overview of the material presented is discussed below:

A New Universe of Data: Explanation of social data, data sources, and the explosive global growth and social platform adoption.

Social Platforms: Drill down into the different types of platform and value proposition surrounding the data. Define the importance of the 10 major platform segments.

1. Sharing platforms
2. Mirco-blogging
3. Publishing platforms
4. Discussion
5. Social networks
6. Live streams
7. Virtual worlds
8. Life cast
9. Social games
10. MMOs

Valuable Data for the Enterprise: Exploration of the five major social data types and their value to business intelligence (BI), each with a use case example and platform example.

A. Sentiment data
B. Behavioral data
C. Social graph data
D. Location data
E. Rich media data

Accessing the Data: Best practices surrounding data integration and governance as it applies to social data in the enterprise; privacy issues with "what not to do" use cases; and marketplaces—Azure, Informatica and others—who are providing social data for analytics.

Social Analytics in the Enterprise: The three areas of social analytics—definitions and applications; drivers for each of these areas; and value definitions.

1. Social BI
2. Social data analytics
3. Social media and network monitoring

Social BI: The five steps to successful social BI, and the definitions and applications in these areas

1. BI for the masses
2. Robust social features
3. Advanced security
4. Highly integrated
5. A meritocracy

Four Steps to the Social BI Process: Definitions and applications coupled with best practice examples.

1. Access
2. Evaluate
3. Collaborate
4. Share

Social data analytics: Use case examples, best practices, tips, and success stories. Go beyond simple Comcast Guy examples to true enterprise return on investment (ROI) and differentiating applications.

Social Media and Network Monitoring: The new breed of BI applications. There are 148 vendors in the space and growing. Application examples and use cases. Discussion of leading vendors and solutions.

Your First Project: Wrap up important themes and best practices supply; add a checklist for success and resources.

As you complete the book and start looking at your own first project, there will be many discussions and meetings, checklists, and proof of concepts that will happen. Our goal is to help you start the journey with this book as a helper in the strategy process. The next book that is being planned in this series is the implementation of social analytics with solution packages and applications.

Best Wishes for a Successful Strategy!

A New Universe of Data

CONTENTS

Social Data Analytics is a fast-growing and critical component of enterprise analytic strategy. Understanding where the data is, how to integrate it into enterprise systems, and what types of analytics can be brought to bear on the data is very important for companies looking to differentiate themselves in the market.

UNDERSTANDING SOCIAL ANALYTIC PLATFORMS

The biggest transformation that we are seeing in the last decade (2002 onwards) is the interest of enterprises large and small to compete for the wallet share of the customer with new and updated products and services that are targeted to satisfy the customer or prospect satisfying their need at the time they are looking at the enterprise set of products and solutions. To accomplish this with result-oriented outcomes, enterprises have strategized the process of understanding the customer by following their behaviors utilizing the social media platforms and machine learning algorithms.

In the new world where globalization and commoditization are the key terms to compete in the market, enterprises need to create and integrate an internal social analytics strategy that will mirror what they do in the outside world, thereby increasing the collaboration between teams, aligning success and quality of insights. Whether it is implementing an internal Twitter-like channel or a Facebook-like community or a Sharepoint-driven collaboration, each of these strategies have specific inputs and outputs, measurements and reports, or dashboards to monitor the same. A good set of examples of goals that organizations today are working in a collaborative fashion to strive toward include the following:

- Create targeted messaging to prospects and customer leads, enabling to convert them to customers. Collaborating on competitive research and campaign marketing to achieve better confidence and trust in forming the customer relationship enables this process and produces better results.
- Improve internal communications and morale of global staff in call-centers and support roles for the organization. This is enabled by implementing a series of collaboration strategies to share data and process information across teams and helps create a transparent information ecosystem. This type of internal data sharing helps in managing customer and prospect situations effectively and efficiently, resulting in satisfied end customers and more happy employees.
- Build brand awareness and track the effectiveness of the current brand campaigns and marketing efforts. This type of exercise was done previously too but did not include competitive intelligence, research articles, online crawlers and content gathered by them, and collaborative comments and gamification-based results from different teams within the enterprise. The availability of the data and the collaboration between different teams have created new ideations and improvisation of existing in-process ideations to leverage the best possible results for the enterprise. This is a big benefit of social analytics in the enterprise and we will be discussing this in multiple case studies and chapters in the book.
- Improved and satisfied customer service and product support. A weak area for all organizations globally, this is a real touchy subject of discussion at C-levels anytime. With the inclusion of social media analytic platforms within the organization, the customer service and support teams have got a transparent customer-focused platform that allows them to share relevant information with the customer and their teams simultaneously to reach decisions and ensure a satisfied

customer and utilize the platform to also create a cross-sell and up-sell opportunity that results in more wallet share.

- Improve your ability to recruit top-notch talent to your team with inclusion of social media analytic platforms. The current and future generations of employees are the generation that is referred to as the "Google" generation. These employees have grown up in a digital world where the boundaries of geographies and social demographics are absent, and the sharing of knowledge and collaboration on solutions is more of the norm. These employees feel more satisfied and are more innovative and productive when the social media platforms used within the enterprise make them improvise the skills they grow up with and utilize through school and college years into the job culture.
- Increase market intelligence by collecting customer feedback, encouraging customer community and collecting information about competitors. These are major influences in the business intelligence decisions and the foundation for the growth of the business and its customers. By including the customer inside your innovation, you will get better market results and more satisfied customers.
- Implement crowdsourcing platforms as a means for completing tasks faster and less expensively than at present. These platforms create and promote better orientation of problem solving, as the situation is open and available to all employees to participate or help solve. The platform drives multiple benefits to the organization: one is the measurement of time reduction and efficiency of problem solving; second is the availability of a number of resources across the organization that was never known before; third is the availability of resources globally if there are regions of operation and their ability to provide a 24/7 model of support to the problem and its solution; and last but not the least the cost savings in the entire solution and its implementation plus the availability of the same for the organization in a knowledge base.

There are many vendors in the social data analytic platform space. Each brings a somewhat unique set of features and functions to the game. Early entrants have been focused primarily on the needs of marketing and public relations teams and often focused on only *monitoring* the social landscape. As an organization's social data analytics strategy evolves from "watching" to a more widely integrated approach, a new set of capabilities is required to meet the needs of enterprise users. Platform functionality will enable a wide range of analytic and functional capabilities, so it is important to make sure the solution you choose for your organization has the platform functionality needed to support action, collaboration, and integration with enterprise data and applications and can support advanced analytic functions.

Platform Functions

What should the key focus areas for platform functionality and implementation be when the organization chooses one or more social analytic platforms. The following features have emerged as some of the key features, and the list can be expanded or modified for any organization's requirements and comfort.

Alerting and Workflow

Social data analytic platforms are gaining traction within enterprise companies and it is vital as more stakeholders become involved that the platform help these professionals to understand the insights that are critical to their organization and take faster action. Alerting and key performance indicator (KPI)–driven metrics have long been included in traditional business intelligence solutions, and they are now finding their way into Social Data Access Platforms (SDAP) solutions. Receiving an email alert or text message is a useful way to interact with social data insights but it's even more successful if the platform combines alerts with workflow functionality that allows users to design business process functions based on the alerts or for alerts to automatically kick off processes based on thresholds and KPIs.

Collaboration

As much as KPIs and alerts help users to take action, collaboration is a key function to add value to workflows and decisions. Most vendors in the social data analytic space are still struggling to provide highly useful collaborative capabilities. As with traditional business intelligence, where bringing a diverse set of skills and insights to a business problem will most often result in a better decision for the organization, overall this is true with social workflows and decisions.

Integration/Application Programming Interfaces

SDAP solutions can't impact the enterprise unless they can be highly and seamlessly integrated with existing analytic platforms and data sources. Many leading business intelligence vendors are incorporating social data analytic capabilities into their business intelligence platforms as a strategy to bring the data and the decision making to a single integrated platform.

Natural Language Processing

Natural language processing (NLP) combines linguistics and artificial intelligence (AI) to enable computers to understand human or natural language input. The business value of NLP is probably obvious. Social data is often information directly created by human input and this data is unstructured in nature, making it nearly impossible to leverage with standard SQL. NLP can make sense of the unstructured data that is produced by social data sources and help to organize it into a more structured model to support SQL-based queries. NLP opens the door for sophisticated analysis of social data and supports text data mining and other sophisticated analytic functions.

These four platform function areas are key foundations for the analytic insights most companies will need to leverage with their social data analytic platform. Alerting, workflows, collaboration, integration, and application programming interfaces (APIs) and NLP engines are important building blocks for strong platforms that strive to support enterprise class needs.

PLATFORM ANALYTIC FUNCTIONS

Below is a list of the type of analytic functions you should demand from the platform you are working with. Not all end users require all of these functions but if you are planning to support a wider array of users within your organization, it's critical to have a strong and flexible analytic foundation within your SDAP application.

Geospatial Analysis

Leveraging the location data of customers, prospects, and communities is a critical capability of a strong social data analytics platform. Understanding the location of a social data element opens the door for creative applications in marketing and service for innovative companies. Examples would include geo-targeted add delivery, regionally focused next best offers, supply chain insight, and more.

Sentiment Analysis

Understanding sentiment within social data is a sophisticated analytic function. It's dependent on the NLP capabilities of the platform and can provide a candid view of how a social community or specific user "feels" about your product, brand, or service. This insight can drive marketing and customer care strategies as well as alert you to growing trends around your service, both positive and negative.

Influence Analysis

Influence is the currency of social data, and it is critically important to understand where influence is within your organization's social sphere. SDAPs with influence analytic capabilities can reveal who is seen as a community or topic leader and give an organization insight into its own influence on topics important to their customers. Identifying influencers and monitoring corporate influence are both critical to successful social data analytic strategies.

Machine Data Analysis

Machine data is often defined as information that is produced by computer systems as processes or functions are executed. An example would be the log file entries that track which pages of a website a browser or group of browsers interact with. This machine data can provide the behavioral insights of a social network user, helping to create a view of what content they are interested in, how long they interact with information, or what advertisement they react to. Leveraging machine data for insight into social interaction and behavior is an exciting point of insight for an organization striving to better understand customers and prospects.

Demographic Analysis

Simple demographic analysis is important, especially to marketing professionals. Some solutions utilize available data via APIs from the social networking platforms supplying the data, whereas others go beyond to leverage NLP technology to determine demographic details based on content and linguistic analysis. Capturing information on gender, age, and ethnicity creates added value in social data. Many originating systems tie the social data to account information for the authors. When this is available for analysis, it is possible to build highly detailed master data on customers and prospects who are socially active.

Brand Affinity

This is a metric utilized by marketing professionals to measure the goodwill created with customers via an organization's branded products. It's similar to sentiment data in that it measure how people feel toward a brand, but in this case is more focused on marketing processes and campaigns. For many marketing professionals, brand affinity analytics is a foundational function to build strategies upon.

Text Analytics

Is a capability that builds on the output from NLP. Once the unstructured social data has been parsed and organized, text mining solutions can analyze the information to identify patterns and trends within the data. Text analytics isn't terribly different from data mining in that it strives to organize the data for analysis and once organized can produce insights otherwise too difficult for people to do manually. Text analytics opens the door for innovative analysis of social data.

We have discussed some of the key areas of focus and the associated analytics that are used or created within the organizations. The questions that come next include who will lead this type of work within the organization, the business sponsors, the governance and policies, the budgets, and measuring the outcomes. The teams for this type of activity should consist of people from all the departments within the organization. The need for inviting all types of talent is to create the community in the organization, which will consist of different types of topics, subjects, issues, and solutions, where the teams that worked in silos for the longest periods of time will find support and ideation from across different aspects of the organization.

One of the biggest challenges that organizations will face, and have been creative to provide solutions for, is the area of governance and policy management around the subject of managing the social media platform. The best recommendation for this exercise in the organization is to follow a combination of program and data governance within the organization. There should be three levels of governance to ensure the right levels of support and visibility in the organization: execution, implementation, and support governance.

Measurement strategies of social media platform implementation for internal usage are different from the implementation for external customer and marketing types of activities. The most common measures are in the areas of subjects discussed, number of participants, number of active discussions, number of problems discussed, number of solutions provided, reduction of time, improvement of efficiencies, increase in collaboration, and usage. While these are some of the common measures, there are several that are created for use in organizations that remain private to the organization and its users.

As we come to the end of the first chapter, we will discuss a case study of the new universe of data and platforms and how an organization deploys a solution providing a robust solution.

CASE STUDY 1 – A NEW UNIVERSE OF DATA

Background

A large multiservice company in the financial services industry discovered in 2007 that campaigns, competitive research, customer relationship management, customer satisfaction index, product propensity, new market acquisition, and overall brand health in print and digital channels were underperforming as programs. The biggest discovery was the fact that new channels of data were becoming available and were providing more intelligence about the trends and factors affecting the behavior of the customer and the market. This new segment of data was creating a digital divide between the current state data and the new external data, from the fact that the digital personas were demonstrating different behaviors compared to the static personas created in-house.

The line of business executives across sales, marketing, and competitive intelligence teams were puzzled by the fact that the new data set was more powerful and was providing critical insights that they were not able to gather from surveys, call center conversations, and other third-party channels.

A study was commissioned to understand these new types of data and their underlying sources of information. The goal of this study was to assess the value of the additional data and its potential capabilities to create stronger decision support architectures for the enterprise to consume.

The Study

To create the most impact on the value of the data, the study included subject matter experts from all the business segments that would be benefited by extending the additional types of data. The common thread that connected these different business units was one area of focus—the customer.

The study categorized the data into the following subsets

- External data—public channels: this includes data available on the Internet for use by anybody. Typical examples include web forums, user groups, and blog posts and discussions, Twitter data, YouTube data (public uploads).
- External data—private channels: this includes data available on the Internet but within a closed loop of networks formed by people based on their personal, work, and other interactions. This data is not available for public use, but by creating and sponsoring such groups, you can harness similar data. Typical examples include LinkedIn Groups, Meetups, Facebook, Flickr, and YouTube (private channels).
- External data—third-party channels: this includes data from aggregators like Nielsen, Gnip, and Datasift and survey data collected by third-party surveys and the like.
- Internal data—external channels: this includes data gathered for competitive research from external suppliers of competitive research data.
- Internal data—internal channels: this includes data from internal channels such as email, surveys, call center conversations, campaign customer segmentation, and other data available in the organization.

All these data artifacts contain hidden nuggets of information than can be vital to the strength of the decision support platform for creating a customer-centric enterprise.

Value of the Data

The hidden value that has been referenced many times includes not just the output from the customer or prospect about your brand but also the long tail that they carry with those expressions. Understanding this long tail is very vital to create a corrective course of action where your brand will not be hit with issues of attrition and loss of revenue repeatedly. The value is associated with the context of the entire sphere of information. Why is context important to understand? We will discuss this next.

Context of the Data

To understand the data available across each of these segments, there are several additional data segments and data attributes that need to be integrated by the enterprise, which were outlined by the study and included the following:

- External
  - Geospatial data—latitude, longitude, zip, city, state, address
  - Weather data
- Internal
  - Campaign data
  - Product data
  - Channel data
  - Customer promotion data
  - Product promotion data

The study further outlined that the organization has to create a customer-focused program aimed at integrating all the data that touches the customer or prospect directly or indirectly, and measures the organization, the customer, competition, and brands using the data harvested from the program. These programs are known as the "Voice of Customer" program in today's social customer relationship management.

To accomplish this program, the following steps need to implemented:

1. Establish listening posts, which are channels of direct and indirect contact for the customer or prospect to voice their concerns, feedback, sentiments, and frustrations. By creating a channel to listen, you take a giant step in understanding the customer or the prospect or the market from a holistic perspective.
2. Extract the data from these listening posts and create a storage architecture to perform a data discovery exercise.
3. Discover the trends and sentiments expressed in these conversations.
4. Integrate the result set into reporting and analytics engines via data integration.
5. Visualize the trends and metrics from the same.
6. Provide the data to relevant business users to derive the intelligence and understand the customer intelligence.

This will help the organization gain a clear understanding from the new data sets what was missing from earlier studies or experiments, which is the context and situational analytics that influence customer behavior.

Understanding Sentiment vs. Context

There are special kinds of software available today called as "Sentiment Analysis" software. These tools capture voice to text and add business rules to process the data, and thereby present wonderful visualizations of sentiments. Additionally, the software will categorize the sentiment tone as positive or negative and the associated conversation or email, the keywords, and trends that led to the inference of the sentiment. While this is a huge step in connecting to the customer, the unfortunate scenario here include the following:

■ The customer sentiment expressed in the conversation is not categorized based on the context. For example, the customer makes the following statement: "I have been very frustrated with a particular service offering and the number of times I had to follow up for the same. I'm not going to engage in the pursuit any further as there is minimal support. I'm very disappointed." In this situation, the sentiment analysis software will help verify that the sentiment is negative, the reason is minimal support, and the customer is disappointed. What the business user will miss here is the big picture that text mining and analytics will look at—customer is unhappy with certain services as he had to follow up and received minimal support; he is unhappy in this context and wishes to cancel the said service. This big picture is contextual in nature, but there are several soft links here, how many more services the customer holds and might cancel, how many other people in his network this customer might influence, or rather how many more customers have expressed such concerns and canceled services. Unless this gap is addressed, the value from the Voice of Customer initiative is deemed primitive.

■ The second listening post is that customers will follow up the conversation with emails. Example: Customer writes an email.

　　■ from: john.doe@myfreecountry.com
　　　to: msvcs@Acme Inc.com
　　　sub: Customer Services Feedback

Dear ACME INC, I have been a customer for the last 30 years of your services. While the relationship has had its share of highs and lows, in recent times your customer services team has been performing very poorly. The response times have been lagging, there is a lack of urgency to close questions, the intent is to sell more services and not address issues. While we appreciate the self-service channels you have opened, this direct channel has deteriorated. Should this trend continue, I will be forced to consider other alternatives.

Sincerely
John Doe"

In this email, there are several key issues and associated sentiments and comparisons. If the customer had written this email and then in a 30-day time frame followed up a call to let ACME INC know that he/she is moving on, there was time to react had the email been parsed and an alert raised on potential attrition.

Why is this important, because if John Doe has 50 friends who hear his story, chances are a loss of all 50 customers or, over a period of time, loss of groups of customers that will lead to revenue loss. Now if John doe were to express this in a Social Media forum, there is brand reputation at stake and more customer attrition.

To increase more actionable insights, you should go beyond just sentiment and perform advanced text mining on an integrated layer of data across multiple channels, including email and social media analytics. The additional steps will help you create the context of the behaviors and its influence, which then not only drives the organization's response but also provides the underlying architecture to create a measurement strategy around the responses, thereby adding better insights; it will provide the organization with ability predict and model customer behavior and be prepared to react better at such situations. The complete set of data and analytics will enable the business user community to better address their knowledge base and learnings, ultimately helping them to create a very positive outcome on their customer interactions.

The study concludes with the following summary:

- To create a customer-centric organization, you need to tap into all the touchpoints of a customer.
- To understand the interaction, you need to go beyond sentiment.
- To derive value, you need to add context.
- To enable all these processes, you must add more layers of data and infrastructure to manage and process the same.

How these companies implemented the system and set up a measurement strategy for success and outcomes will be discussed in case studies in the next few chapters of this book.

Social Analytics in the Enterprise

The social enterprise is a collaborative ecosystem that consists of an integration of social analytics, business intelligence, and decision support architecture. The biggest outcome for the enterprise that adopts this kind of a platform is it evolves as a flat and smart organization with internal and external transparencies as needed, and it provides the entire organization a uniform board of understanding users, prospects, competition, and markets. The other benefit that is available is the fact that change is the only constant and connectedness helps the customer or prospect understand the change from the organization. What are the key success criteria for this change to happen, or in other words, "What enables this?" There are several factors to consider, and the most important that need to be considered are as follows:

- Culture
- Leadership
- Technology

These factors need to be implemented in "enabling natural human interactions." After leadership and an inclusive and open culture are in place, we can deploy social technology that will enable enterprises to become true social beings. The technology layer empowers and enables us to be more agile and organize for the market conditions in real time, thus laying the foundation to become customer centric. It also allows us access to better insights, so we have meaningful, deep, and informed interactions with our internal and external ecosystems.

The beauty of social networks and social media lies in data analytics and insights that are provided by the data aspects. Each and every interaction creates a data point and builds upon a pattern of interactions that enrich the knowledge repository and creates analytics, which allows for better and smarter future interactions. Let's consider a few examples, from an e-commerce perspective, Amazon incorporates user behavioral data into its sales recommendation engine in real time; *behavior* here includes activities on the website and the clickstream it produces on products, reviews, time spent on a page or a product, switch between pages of same and different products, and more. The benefit of integrating the movements as it happens into the real-time recommendation engines is the ability to stay consistent with changing thoughts of the prospect or customer. The integration is not simple and does take several pieces of data to be stitched together into the algorithms for producing the final outcome.

> Businesses relatively experienced with social business perspectives and techniques are seeing innovative opportunities to improve internal business processes and techniques through better access to insights and pattern detection, and have been able to achieve a higher degree of customer satisfaction and prospect confidence by aligning to their requirements with the integration of social media analytics into the business analytics of the organization.

While the integration of social media and analytics is explored in later chapters, we need to understand the overall benefits from the integration and how any enterprise can start this journey with the outcomes established from the following discussion in this chapter.

Connect—The first phase of social analytics and data integration within the enterprise starts with the connect phase or stage of operations. The typical empowerments and enablements established in the enterprise with deployment of collaboration and communication platforms include the following:

- Conversations—From top executives to call center and external sales support staff, all employees and staff within the organization can stay connected with collaboration and conversations.

- Content—Share content including files, pictures, and videos to keep vital connects in conversations.
- Private Messages—Conversations can include public and private messages. This is useful in the call center of today.
- Notifications—Keep automatic updates with notifications on topics.
- Share—A good empowerment for call center users specifically, you can share relevant context-based content for transparency between you and your customers.

Engage—The second stage of empowerment by implementing social analytics is engagement. This within the organization creates an excellent set of activities providing positive outcomes. The activities in this stage include the following:

- Groups—Internal projects and programs can be connected with groups of people working for or participating in these projects using collaboration suites and sharing content and aligning the search of these content details with semantic frameworks, taxonomies, and ontologies.
- Challenges—There are several challenges and opportunities that exist for all organizations, some are solved by the brightest and best within the organization teams, there are some challenges that need to be solved quickly, here is the best-use case for social analytics and its implementation, by publishing the challenges and the list of opportunities that can be solved within the collaboration suites of the organization, you can tap into the creativity of your entire organization to brainstorm new ideas or tackle complex problems. You can solicit instant feedback and watch the best solutions rise to the top within the organization. Several big-name companies have adopted this technique, providing employee satisfaction as the best return on investment (ROI) for the organization.
- Projects—Several projects within organizations require critical steps to be managed to ensure success, and there is dependence on these projects—not to forget the patches and updates that are needed to fix issues, certify the product on new hardware or software, and updates for the services catalog or any other activity that pulls away resources or introduces delays. To ensure maximum information sharing and also transparency in terms of resources and where they are, the social analytics types of data platforms with visualizations always help. In terms of productivity, a leading software development company says they improved 27% year over year after they adopted this exercise compared to prior years. Another large call center services company improved internal knowledge sharing and created more visible opportunities that were offered to customers to solve complex situations, thus increasing loyalty while improving employee satisfaction.

- Thanks—How do you honor someone for their tireless work and especially if the work was more in terms of saving an opportunity while not worrying about the time and the hours spent? The best opportunities are by thanking them and recognizing their special efforts. You can do this on an internal Twitter, Instagram, or Snapchat type of platform, which will bring more collaboration, and the gamification aspects of these approaches also allow several employees to add to the recognition and thanks. This also provides the enterprise an opportunity to acknowledge these employees at a quarterly meeting and some even get promotions based on these types of outcomes.
- Town Halls—A popular concept among startups and smaller companies is the town halls where the executives, midlevel managers, and employees meet to exchange and discuss ideas and innovations. With the implementation of social media platforms within the enterprise, the town halls can be conducted in a virtual environment with the same capabilities and more geographic reach. Copies of town halls can be viewed from saved versions and also used for ensuring traceability of conversations. Many companies are now using this technique to implement training for the employees and new hires.
- External Data Feeds—Knowing your customer, prospect, and competition at the same time is a great thought, and we can now get this data from external data feeds that can be tracked, purchased, and interactively collected. There are many companies specializing in data collection and listening post management that will provide services for data gathering. The data from this collection is useful for market research, competitive research, and marketing and campaign management.

Discover—A social analytics platform within the enterprise provides employees with benefits, including organizational structure, profiles, and search for hashtags, social media presence, and more. These features are useful in managing a diverse team spread across different areas of the world.

- Organization—Look up the organization chart and details in a few clicks. Connect with internal folks within and outside your team on topics of common interest and discuss details as appropriate in these communities.
- Profile—Profiles are of great interest to anybody in any organization, especially if you have external social media profiles that are different from whom you are within the organization. A social media and analytics platform provides a great linkage to connect the external and internal data points connected with your profile. This profile availability as a feature has helped organizations to identify opportunities where they can leverage an employee's perspective and

seek the right kind of help and advice as needed. This feature can be extended to call center and operations support, benefiting the organization in many areas.

- Search—You are looking at the markets and find interesting tags that link your company and competition in comparisons and predictions. The search feature will provide a suitable set of results including hashtags, context, links, and more details. This feature is appreciated by teams such as competitive research and market research who relied on surveys and third-party results for a long period of time. You can add auto listen and store attributes that create content and push it to you and also to others in the community who are interested in participating in this content and its usage in the organization.

With features that help you discover more of the organization and align the teams, the interest in social analytics and its adoption within the enterprise has increased in the last few years.

The Prospective Future—Once a social enterprise has gained a critical mass in adoption toward social, it can utilize the real-time data streams of multiple social interactions to have the ability to do the following:

- Find better expertise—How many of us work with someone who is also an expert in another unrelated field but was never recruited nor has ever participated officially in that field? Their participation on social networks, internal and external, allows us to have an ability to detect and identify their uncataloged capabilities and interests. HR departments are utilizing this ability to recruit internally first for emerging areas of interest for the business.
- Increase knowledge sharing—Being able to efficiently capture and analyze information and reutilize knowledge assets has exponential benefits to sales, marketing, support, and product units within the organization. Better knowledge sharing also allows quicker revenue recognition and unnecessary costs associated with inefficient tactics based on poor data. Reutilizing of assets is an immediate positive ROI benefit.
- Gain better market insights—"No matter how big you are, there are always more smarter people on the outside, than on the inside, of your business." A common challenge faced by businesses of all sizes is an inability to understand the evolving needs of existing and potential new customers and markets. Utilizing social monitoring tools to "listen" and understand the social media space allows businesses to become smarter by identifying trends and gain deep insights into competitive, industry, and customer ecosystems. Imagine launching a new product with deep insights in competitive landscape, positioning, branding, messaging, and pricing.

- Improved risk management—Imagine being able to identify potential customer service issues before they become a viral topic on Twitter? Real-time social analytics allows businesses to mitigate potential risks and utilize the medium to amplify the positives. Immediate positive impact on speedy communications of new or revised safety policies, regulations, and improved ability to address crisis scenarios are often seen by social enterprises.
- Better process management—Minimize or eliminate delays through knowledge sharing, tagging, and trend monitoring. If we know that a certain device or software app is causing a specific issue, then we have an ability to address it faster and more efficiently. From a personal social interaction to a machine-generated social interaction, the analytics allow us to identify the key performance indicators (KPIs) that matter the most to a social enterprise.

The need for social analytics for business has grown out of fundamental changes in how our business operates today in the connected economy. Customer preferences and markets are evolving faster than ever. Use of real-time analytics in social interactions, files, and other digital assets in our ecosystem allows a social enterprise to identify patterns and relevant data points that provide it with the ability to organize for the real-time connected economy. That is the true agile social enterprise.

SUMMARY

A global energy giant faced the challenge of enhancing collaboration and knowledge sharing across its global workforce. The enterprise head of *Community Networks* used a formula of experimentation and sound methodology to deliver a new platform to more than 70,000 employees in more than 68 countries. Identifying key elements of company culture and business requirements provided the foundation for the company's new internal platform efforts. The organization has experienced benefits ranging from brand recognition to increased innovation and a reduced carbon footprint.

PUT EMPLOYEES FIRST

Before talking to vendors, before doing a pilot, and before ever looking at technology, the executive first wanted to understand how employees work. The goal was to learn how communities could be formed around shared interests and culture.

As the leader looked across the company, it became clear that departments like R&D, technology, and engineering could most benefit from a collaboration platform. "We have so much expertise and so many different products." The employees in these business areas could capitalize greatly from having a combined knowledge base.

The team continued to work with informal networks, such as their Six Sigma organization, to see how employees connected by interest and separated by geography worked together. Developing a better understanding of how employees work and which departments could benefit the most, the team felt comfortable developing requirements, selecting tools that would meet those requirements, and launching pilots.

PILOT, EXPERIMENT, LEARN

At the time this project kicked off, talking about "social networks" at the organization was unpopular. However, there were individual initiatives through social networking sites (e.g., LinkedIn, Facebook). All along, the leader knew she would have to experiment in order to put together a business case she could take to the rest of the company. During this time, she and her team used experimental pilots to continue to understand business needs and requirements. "We started with five pilots, using communities with different drivers and maturity levels," she stated when asked about the initial phases of work.

Through the multiple pilots, the organization's collaborative needs began to emerge. There was a need to enable online communities, but what also became apparent was the need to update the piecemealed, dated IT environment.

While the team was temporarily without a formal business case, they were never without key leadership backing. All the key executives, CFO, CIO, SVP of HR, VP of Education & University, and SVP of Strategy, were looped in from the beginning, regularly updated on the pilots' progress and challenges. The HR leader realized that having executive backing early on would prove critical to the team's success. "Our strategy was to start with the believers and with sponsors that have business challenges where collaboration is needed."

ALSTOM'S PILLARS OF COLLABORATION

Armed with executive backing and a better understanding of employee culture and business requirements, the HR team put together the organization's Collaborative Way program. Providing the foundation for the go-forward plan, the Collaborative Way was founded on three pillars: (1) building a collaborative IT environment; (2) improving people management and new ways of working; and (3) establishing common methodologies and tools for communities.

- Collaborative IT environment
  Continuing with the experimentation theme, the organization started down the formal tool selection path by piloting externally hosted community forums. Initially limited to all internal University employees, the pilot's immediate success quickly created demand from all parts of the company. Beyond just the forums, demand for other functionalities grew as well. With the help of the organization's CIO, the HR team quickly added separate wiki and blogging applications that were available company-wide.
  "While successful, hosting these tools externally was not an acceptable long-term solution. At that time, everything had to be internalized, hosted on our servers." In addition to moving the tools into the IT environment, there was a need to combine the tools into a single platform. "We let people use the technology as a sandbox, now we are moving to a completely integrated environment," says the HR leader in terms of what the accomplishments were.

- People management and new ways of working
  When it came to employee education, the internal University already had the processes it needed; it was a matter of adapting the content to address tool how-to's, as well as community and collaboration best practices. The company also created a collaboration competency and built a series of guides on how to run collaborative events and meetings. "We thought that collaboration could be seen as only virtual or by using technology, but we wanted all meetings to be more collaborative." The HR team and its leader wanted to emphasize the importance of shifting to a mindset of collaboration. As the tools are only a means to an end, they wouldn't be utilized if the culture remained silted.

- Common Community Framework
  With employees spread all over the world, the internal University needed to come with a common framework it could use to guide community owners through community setup and management. The goal was to have a menu of tools and processes so anyone looking to create a community could be autonomous and use the menu in a self- service manner. This was already a big culture shift. To complement the menu and walk community owners through key decisions, the team developed the "Community Lifecycle" and a toolkit. "The Community Lifecycle governs a community from inception all the way through shut down."
  While each community would be customized to support its individual needs, owners still needed help evangelizing the benefit of a community, eliciting participation and picking which tools would best meet their requirements.

To help spread the word of what the HR leader and her team were doing, the team created an "Introduction to Communities in the Organization" video. The video would be played to kick off all large company events. Once the video piqued user interest, they would contact the team and could apply the lifecycle methodology to help the community get up and running. This video is also available on external public channels like YouTube, Dailymotion, or Slideshare.

GOVERNANCE

We made it very clear from the beginning that our communities should abide by three basic rules:

1. Collaboration is business related
2. Collaboration should not be anonymous
3. Activities within these platforms should be monitored, not censored.

The leaders knew that having a developed governance model would help gain leadership buy-in. "The governance helps a lot. We are still in a culture where authority has its importance. Governance helped us to set the scene and build the foundation."

At the organization, governance was an executive concern, but it was addressed satisfactorily with pilot experimentation. At the same time the team was setting the governance, they were gathering best practices and success stories from the pilot. One of these best practices became mandatory: each community must have a Community Leader, someone to monitor and follow community life.

The Community Leader drives activity in the community, stimulating and maintaining the group dynamic. He or she requests resources as needed, coordinates meetings and deliverables, and liaises between members and the Community Sponsor. The Sponsor is outside the community but still supports and promotes the community to the outside world, and provides strategic direction and new missions. The Sponsor provides resources as needed and participates in the validation of community recommendations. And should a community become inactive, the organization had the foresight to build in metrics and triggers that would prompt community shutdown. "If there is no activity within six months, if people aren't motivated to participate or if the sponsor becomes disengaged . . . we can make that decision confidently."

Governance was also evident at a departmental level where roles were clearly defined. IT was responsible for building the enterprise collaborative environment; HR examined the way in which they recruited, developed, and rewarded collaboration; and everyone involved was responsible for developing a common framework for community planning, training, development, and roll-out.

HOW TO MEASURE SUCCESS

ROI and KPIs get a lot of buzz in the e2.0 world. The HR leader, like many other practitioners, noted that KPIs and ROI metrics were difficult to ascertain. "We started to measure the activities through the tools, we called it a dashboard . . . but frankly the measured metrics do not reflect collaboration, but rather activity which is essentially meaningless." After a few months, the leader directed the reporting to focus more on return on experience (ROE) than ROI. Documented interviews with successful community managers were initially posted on the corporate intranet; now the team conducts and posts video testimonials.

One such successful community is the 1,000-member Global Field Service Network. The community is composed of employees from all around the world who have expertise in the organization's power plants. "They created a pool of people who travel globally. In the low activity period, they participate in the community and by transferring knowledge."

SUCCESS IS MORE THAN METRICS

There are no concrete metrics that capture the organizational success. However, they believe it has experienced multiple benefits from its collaboration roll-out, many of them emergent. The first is what the company calls the "employee lifecycle." The organization has seen a boost to its brand among potential employees. "It's helped attract some new candidates," explains the HR leader. The Collaborative Way approach has received attention at conferences. "It's quite modern compared to other major industrial companies with Latin culture."

Alstom now has a new understanding of what it takes to be successful in its highly federated, but collaborative, culture. HR is now looking at augmenting the skill set it looks for in developing leaders or managers. It's not only about functional expertise but about the behaviors you want to assess, evaluate, and reward.

Collaboration has also sparked innovation at the organization. Ideas are being shared more readily than before. The Innovation Management System Community realized that they didn't have a community for managers. "They gathered 100 managers facing the same problems, and now they're collaborating on ways they can all help the organization be more innovative." This community engaged the VP of Strategy and is now working on developing a new approach to improve innovation inside the organization.

A final area in which the organization is seeing great benefit, and in line with their corporate social responsibility efforts, is a reduction in their carbon footprint. By implementing a Cisco Telepresence© solution, with each virtual meeting held, the enterprise is measuring and reducing its CO_2 emissions.

WHAT'S NEXT?

There are still challenges. There is an element of management resistance that the company is experiencing. "Managers want to know that the information being shared in these communities is accurate." Executive leaders believe that a continued focus on user education and change management can help show that not only is the information accurate but that communities are self-regulating, weeding out the inaccurate information.

The internal University is by no means finished in bringing collaboration and capabilities to employees. The company is currently working on rolling out an educational video–sharing platform solution (their privately owned University Tube) to enable social learning and knowledge sharing.

Today employees can record and share short, but valuable, educational content. "Think about it, we have nearly 100K trainers in the company." For those about to embark on an Enterprise 2.0 initiative, the executive leader has advice. "It's not about the tools; it's about their usage and the mindset." She warns against rolling out tools if you don't first change the culture to one of collaboration. To that end, she suggests getting management buy-in early on so that employees know it's acceptable to share knowledge through these new tools. "You can have the best tool in the world...it will be useless if you don't have adopters. So don't think about the tool, think about how it impacts the organization."

As seen from the case study, harnessing social analytic initiatives and its approaches provides great benefits to any organization. To completely build upon these initiatives and how to leverage technologies, there are discussions in the next chapters and case studies in the book.

Social Business Intelligence

CONTENTS

The years 2006–2013 have played a significant role in the business intelligence and analytics industry and the current times are continuing to disrupt and evolve the industry to a dynamic future. The focus of this chapter is the discussion of the integration of social analytics and business intelligence, to create a platform that provides a holistic insight into details beyond the metrics of the reports, including the how, why, who, what, where, and when of the details surrounding the metrics. Social analytics by itself has started gaining immense focus and is becoming adopted as an enterprise standard, but there is still a great deal of misunderstanding as to how it can be used effectively by business teams and users across organizations. The new-age range of business intelligence and analytics tools have all provided an application programming interface (API)–driven frameworks to connect Social analytics as another data source to reports, dashboards, metrics, and analytics. How do we leverage this architecture and deliver more insights to the business users, thereby increasing the data-driven decision support architecture usage and adoption?

To understand the integration and usability, let us revisit social media and analytics first. Social media has evolved from being introduced as a cultural facilitator, to a very real business tool. Social networks powerfully differentiate themselves from earlier Internet marketing channels in that on a daily basis, they gather, parse, and provide commercially valuable demographic data of the end user in usable formats to business users and organizations.

Social media analytics today describes wide range of services, communications, and evolutions that take place throughout cyberspace. While the phrase is descriptive, think of it as one of many views of the Internet. An important recognition to provide here is our distinction of social media as a subset of a larger business intelligence and analytics where the components, various platforms, protocols, and devices are all different aspects of a platform providing the data visualization, impact, and connectivity.

The biggest attention on the phrase social media is its potential to bring larger customer bases to smaller organizations that produce for increasingly niche markets, to make target customer metrics more granular and to enable the empowerment of the end user and client, giving them a sense of governance over how the products that serve them are created.

The fundamental data that social media analytics brings to the table is the reason we are seeing this shift; the ability to look at social networks, location, real-time user behavior, and demographic data is very useful and can help in decision support.

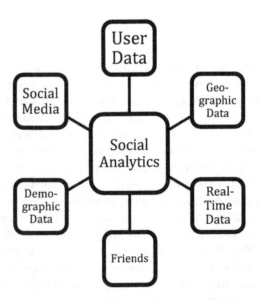

FIGURE 3.1 Social analytics ecosystem. *Source: Krishnan Research 2008.*

In 2007 researchers from Rice University, University of Maryland, and Max Planck Institute for Software Systems analyzed what characteristics of very large online social networks made them so successful. The study makes an important point, that while web pages are based on content, online social networks are based on users. The conclusion of the study is also fascinating, because the researchers found that the most trustworthy "nodes," or members, of the network are those users who established the largest number of "friends" within the online network, establishing themselves as close to the "core" of that social network as possible. This means that the closer to the core of a social network that you are, the faster you're able to propagate information out to a wider segment of the network. This is exactly the kind of opportunity that organizations need to look for establishing a customer- or user-centric business approach. The core characteristics of social media and analytics can be described as follows:

1. **User-based:** Before social networks like Facebook or MySpace became the norm, websites were based on content that was updated by one user and read by Internet visitors. The flow of information was in a single direction, and the Webmaster, or writer, determined the direction of future updates. Online social networks, on the other hand, are built and directed by users themselves. Without the users, the network would be an empty space filled with empty forums, applications, and chat rooms. Users populate the network with conversations and content. The direction of that content is determined by **anyone** who takes part in the discussion. This is what makes social networks so much more exciting and dynamic for Internet users.

2. **Interactive:** Another characteristic of modern social networks is the fact that they are so interactive. This means that a social network is not just a collection of chat rooms and forums anymore. Websites like Facebook are filled with network-based gaming applications, where you can play poker together or challenge a friend to a chess tournament. These social networks are quickly becoming a pastime that more people are choosing over television—because it's more than just entertainment, it's a way to connect and have fun with friends.

3. **Community-driven:** Social networks are built and thrive from community concepts. This means that just like communities or social groups around the world are founded on the fact that members hold common beliefs or hobbies, social networks are based on the same principle. Within most modern online social networks today, you'll find sub-communities of people who share commonalities, such as alumni of a particular high school, or an animal welfare group. Not only can you discover new friends within these interest-based communities, but you can also reconnect with old friends that you lost contact with many years ago.

4. **Relationships:** Unlike the websites of the past, social networks thrive on relationships. The more relationships that you have within the network, the more established you are toward the center of that network. Like the concept most pyramid schemes are focused on, within online social networks, the concept really works in a powerful way. When you have just 20 contacts and you publish a note or an update on that page, that content proliferates out across a network of contacts and subcontacts that's much larger than you might realize.

5. **Emotion over content:** Another unique characteristic of social networks is the emotional factor. While websites of the past were focused primarily on providing information to a visitor, the social network actually provides users with emotional security and a sense that no matter what happens, their friends are within easy reach. Whether suffering through divorce, breakup, or any other family crisis, people are finding that the ability to jump online and communicate directly with a circle of friends provides a great deal of support in an otherwise unmanageable situation.

Looking at the data and the core characteristics, we can definitely bring the user-based data and create integration with data warehouse and business intelligence layers of the enterprise. The reason for adding the data warehouse in the integration is to ensure that if trending and statistical algorithms need to be executed, it is better to create persistence storage. If no persistence is needed, then integrating at the business intelligence layer is fantastic.

The trick and area of development that needs to be created as a framework or a blueprint is on how to generate the integration in such a way that it is reliable and measurable. The Internet serves as a connector between the enterprise and the end user, and this connectivity from the business cycle is just beginning to define itself. While it is clear that there are a few gaps, we have extensive opportunities for companies that can facilitate efficient flow and interpretation of data along these roads while demonstrating tangible ROI.

The pulse of ongoing dialog within social networks/media can be tapped to reveal community and consumer sentiment to a degree that traditional poll/focus group measurements cannot, particularly with regards to authenticity, the proximity to how a client or customer feels outside of a controlled environment. The consumer feedback is digitally available today and easily parse-able in a way that is suitable for business intelligence and operations processes to integrate, providing ongoing optimization.

Social media has evolved over the last decade from just being a portal-based business to an interactive user-oriented and cloud-based business. The following are the key impacts that we will need to focus on when we integrate the social analytics and business intelligence data.

SOCIAL ANALYTICS AND BUSINESS INTELLIGENCE INTEGRATION

The five foundational components that provide data for creating the social business intelligence platform, that is, social media, marketing strategy, business intelligence, customer relationship management (CRM), and internal business processes, shown in figure 3.2 have been evolving on their own unique paths for the last few years while at the same time looking across the bow at other parallel fields of development and then converging with them to the extent that they provide value.

With the advancements of format commonality and data availability, there is now a great degree of interrelatedness and this provides the organization data connectedness to decide which mix is appropriate to their business requirements.

Each of these components relates to one or more of the others in a functional way, and integrating them at the right level of granularity and details adds value and efficiency to the organization, with insights that will result in positive gains for its products/services and operations. Let's quickly define each of these terms in order to be clear and also to see how they are different from each other.

FIGURE 3.2 The five foundational pillars of social analytics and business intelligence integration.
Source: Krishnan Research 2008.

Social Media

It is through the social media that individuals and companies use websites, and which serves as the primary source of content for the end user. Because of this, gaining credibility is not only a matter of supplying good content but having good social interaction. A common starting mistake is to view social media as a platform for email blasts and "campaigns" rather than as a process of facilitated, trusted, contextualized, and personalized communication channel. Another mistake that enterprises have stumbled upon is to attend to customer needs and issues via social media; it is not wise to do so.

Social media can be considered more of a broadcast and participation, and even lead generation media. The host of the service determines all the data interactions and access rights, which when used effectively can create more customer- and prospect-focused business activity.

Social media relates to other business components in that it informs them with a real-time immediacy that has been previously unavailable. This has huge potential for a new set of marketing metrics.

The Internet is now brimming with companies willing to parse through, store, and interpret your social media interactions, each of them with a different level of granularity, reliability, and cost.

The top social media sites that have extensive APIs and can provide data through authorized partners are listed in the table.

Social Media Site	Strengths	Weaknesses
Facebook	By far, the biggest user base. Powerful API allows for understanding user sentiment and demographics.	Unlike a search engine, users don't come here with a purchase mindset. Ad revenues and stock price reflect this.
Twitter	Short simple messages allow for a large number of data points. Strong, loyal, and active community. Many third-party apps.	Though more easily readable, short messages contain less data.
YouTube	Biggest video site by far. Powerful API can reveal user trends.	Used less as a communication platform than Twitter or Facebook. Comments on a video tend to be less conversational.
Pinterest	Visually attractive. Loyal users. Large amount of content.	Majority of content is pictures. Comments relate to those pictures. Thus more difficult to determine context.

Social Media Site	Strengths	Weaknesses
Meetup	Focused on creating and scheduling meetups coupled with the API, one can locate trends in a geographic area.	Smaller user base.
Google +	Advanced technologies, integrated into its email platform. Loyal knowledgeable people.	Less teen and young adult oriented. Growing slowly.
Tumblr	Great for following trends among bloggers. Can give great insight into trendsetters.	Smaller user base. Less appealing than Twitter or Facebook for direct promotion. Long-term planning required.
LinkedIn	Professional network. Ideal for determining industry trends.	Limits on access. More exclusive behavior in general.

CRM

CRM focuses on service, retention, sales, and lead generation. This is the component that addresses the customer on a more one-to-one level and speaks more specifically on customer-related issues such as terms of service, pricing, email lists, and the actual sale.

It differs from the social media component in that it is less promotional and participatory and more actionable. It is the mechanism through which deals are closed and customers receive hard goods.

Social media informs CRM as to what actions need to be taken, and CRM uses social media as a way to broadcast participation and messages that pertain to both current and potential customers.

By making social media a CRM component, potential customers can have a firsthand look at the company they will be dealing with should they decide to make a purchase.

Marketing Strategy

Marketing Strategy indicates the methods and tactics used to gain the attention that leads to sales. Both social media and CRM efforts need to rely on a comprehensive approach to the customer that is built on the company's mission statement and long-term goals. Without this, the flood of information from a constant stream of services coming online will overwhelm the marketing approach and reduce it to little more than a scramble to answer everyone, one-to-one, in real time.

Marketing to an audience that has this one-to-one potential does not obligate you to speak to everyone. Having these tools requires you to "choose your battles" for maximum return.

In the same way that a short-tempered employee can embarrass his whole organization with one rude tweet, a well-trained staff can create large positive waves of goodwill simply by focusing attention on a situation and audience that has high and positive visibility.

Locating these spots on the web, these communities and times of day is the function of marketing strategy. Both social media and CRM interactions help to inform this.

Business Intelligence

Business intelligence is the ability to dig into data that have been acquired through disparate channels and business activities and then identify trends, opportunities, and areas where efficiency can be improved.

As stated above, social media and CRM are used to inform the long-term marketing strategy. The problem is the huge volume of data coming from both channels. This is where business intelligence comes in. Business intelligence compiles, parses, and interprets this data into reports and forms that are consumable for marketers and strategists.

What business intelligence cannot do is change the quality of the data coming in. There does need to be a starting point so that an organization feels comfortable that incoming information is useable by the company, which it comes from the target audience. Locating these sources of useful data is one of the services offered by various consulting companies or dedicated marketing staff.

In addition, effective business intelligence requires a staff or consultant who knows what to look for and how to find it—a person who knows how to read data in a way that provides business value.

The majority of social media marketing and enterprise marketing companies providing service today are in this space. That is, collecting data from your interactions and then interpreting it. They do this for you, provide tools to that end or, as consultants, provide the strategy, recommendations, and support for you to implement. Such companies define themselves, and their cost structure, based on how comprehensive the data collection is as well as how deep the data analysis goes.

Because this is an evolving area, there are many companies that struggle to define what it is that they do and how to integrate their offerings into your business process.

Simple free services count how many Twitter followers you have or how many times someone mentions your name, leaving it up to you to interpret the data.

Other companies collect data from Twitter, Facebook, and YouTube (or another collection of sites) and provide some interpretation for a monthly fee. Still other companies do above, with a more robust database implementation, a deeper view plus historical analysis.

Finally, companies like SAP, Oracle, and IBM provide the means to process huge amounts of information using highly complex analyses.

- At the low end, there is no marketing and branding consulting included.
- At the middle tier, such consulting is offered for additional cost and, beyond this, various companies are balanced in different ways.
- At the high end, it is assumed that you are paying big bucks and so will have support available for the organization.

The four components can be harnessed into business intelligence with data integration, and interesting metrics can be completed.

Some of the most common metrics include the following:

- Number of comments posted to your blog posts (on average)
- Number of blog page views
- Number of RSS feed subscribers
- Number of mentions in blogs, tweets, videos, Facebook pages, etc.
- Number of Twitter followers
- Number of Twitter retweets
- Number of Facebook friends
- Number of Facebook fans
- Number of Diggs, and number of mentions on other social bookmarking sites
- Number of YouTube channel subscribers
- Number of YouTube friends
- Number of comments posted to your videos on YouTube and other video-sharing sites
- Number of podcasts downloaded or played
- Number of podcast subscribers
- Number of downloads of free content (such as white papers and free reports)
- Number of customer reviews on Amazon and other consumer sites
- Total number of monthly conversations
- Number of brand evangelists
- Number of brand detractors
- Number of key influencers discovered
- Number of sales leads generated through social tech
- Number of website visitors referred from social tech links

- Amount of time visitors spend on website and social tech pages
- Number of social technology connections who become sales leads
- Ratio of social technology connections who convert into sales
- Total number of connections across social tech sites

There may also be social sites specific to your industry, and you should be monitoring your presence on these as well.

In time, consider tracking more sophisticated metrics, such as the following:

- Ratio of comments to blog posts
- Ratio of tweets to retweets
- Month-over-month growth velocity rate of Twitter followers
- Month-over-month growth velocity rate of Facebook fans
- Month-over-month growth velocity rate of RSS feed subscribers
- Month-over-month growth velocity rate of YouTube channel subscribers
- Number of average followers of your Twitter followers

Measuring Outcomes

The goal of social analytics and business intelligence integration is not to win a "feel good" contest; it's to increase your bottom line. Therefore, you must also use standard organizational analytics in order to set a baseline for where you stand at the time you begin implementing social media strategies. The metrics to consider include the following:

- Gross sales
- Number of sales transactions per month
- Rate of sales growth
- Amount of average sale
- Number of new customers per month
- Amount of new customer revenue per month
- Length of sales cycle
- Lifetime value of a customer
- Cost of each sales lead
- Sales lead conversion percentage
- Cost to acquire a new customer using established marketing channels (TV ads, search engine marketing, ads in Yellow Pages, etc.)
- Your brand's market share
- Percentage of customer satisfaction
- Percentage of customer retention
- Refund rate
- Number of customer referrals

The integration of social and business intelligence together will help us create different perspectives and provide a baseline for creating an intelligent enterprise.

CASE STUDY

SMS Campaign: Route 66 Harley-Davidson

A 12-day SMS campaign using Route 66 as the keyword for Harley-Davidson Route 66 dealership. The goal of the SMS campaign was to create visibility with current customers and prospects. This would in turn lead to word of mouth sharing of information and eventually help in a better flow of revenue. The dates of the campaign were between December 12 and 24, 2011.

Call to Action

Consumers were encouraged to text the keyword RT66 to 55678 in the campaign and the actual count of consumers doing unique and all texts were reported on the hour for the campaign.

Objective

Route 66 Harley-Davidson wanted to maintain its visibility with current customers and add new customers and revenue through a holiday promotion.

Strategy

The goal for 7 Media Group's services for Route 66 Harley-Davidson was to promote products and increase sales to existing and new members of their mobile club. Membership in Route 66's mobile club was promoted through its social media campaign, in-store marketing, and previous customers of the dealership. Members then received daily alerts offering a 20 percent discount on a different merchandise item each day. This increased customer awareness of the merchandise inventory and drew more customers into the store during a time of the year when sales are typically slower.

RESULTS

The dealership had a significant increase in sales of the specific items discounted during the campaign period. For example, the sale of T-shirts purchased on T-shirt Day was over 250 percent more than a normal day. High-dollar items also saw increased sales. On Helmet Day, the number of helmets sold with the 20 percent discount equaled the number sold for the entire previous week; and on Leather Jacket Day, seven leather jackets were sold at the 20 percent discount, representing a 16 percent increase over jacket sales the previous week. These numbers also represented an increase in dealership traffic.

Lessons learned

"The 12 Days of Christmas campaign provided Route 66 Harley-Davidson increased sales, increased dealership traffic, and an increase in its mobile club membership," said the marketing manager for the dealership. "This promotion continued the success of its mobile marketing that previously helped drive traffic to sponsored events, expanded membership in its mobile club, and increased entries in contests," he added.

CASE STUDY: A GOLDMINE OF INSIGHTS

This case study discusses how a large enterprise software maker created a new intelligence platform by combining internal organization insights with these different nuggets of data, and turned social data into enterprise asset and delivered value.

The background at the enterprise was there were 30-plus systems that catered to providing customer support and information exchange with no integration across the systems. The bigger challenge was the growth of multiple communities around the different products that were developed and sold by the enterprise with minimal involvement from a corporate perspective. The overall image the enterprise had created in the market was that of superior products and inferior support and customer-centric approaches.

The biggest issues faced by the enterprise included

- Lack of knowledge about individual customers
- Lack of integrated information about the engagement of the customers for different products and services
- Lack of insights on revenue situation with respect to support and maintenance revenues
- Lack of insights on social media and its impact on the enterprise, brand, products, and services

The other issues that needed data from these insights included

- Competitive research
- Product innovation
- Performance management
- Channel management

In addition to the internal issues, the competition was ahead of the enterprise in its ability to connect with customers across social media channels and, in the words of many comparison studies, their enterprise lacked the ability to connect with the "Gen Z" and "Millennial" generation of users.

The enterprise decided to adopt a blue ocean strategy approach to creating an approach to answer all these questions by combining the data across internal and external sources. The strategy was conceptualized in five distinct phases

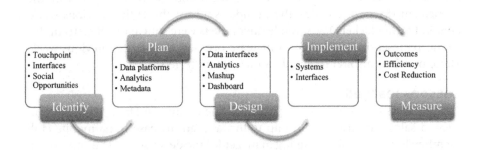

These phases helped the organization to create a roadmap-based approach where the different teams using the 30-plus applications, the associated data, and the new teams that were focused on social networking aspects were aligned into one program. Once the team members were aligned, the critical phases and finer details were defined as follows

- Identify the customer touchpoints
  - Where are all the areas where the customer data is available
    - Within the enterprise
    - Outside the enterprise
  - What are the different interfaces that customers interact with the enterprise
  - What are the different product channels that are known to exist
    - Within the enterprise
    - Outside the enterprise
- Identify the product touchpoints
  - Where are all the areas that are product focused
    - Within the enterprise
    - Outside the enterprise
  - Which products consume maximum resources to support
  - What are the different social media channels where the products are supported by external parties known or unknown to the organization
- Identify the market situation in terms of brand and reputation and understand the customer's sentiments
- Identify the competitor through the eyes of the customer
- Analyze the support provided by the communities of customers versus the enterprise

Once the data from these different aspects are collected, the next step is to analyze the common trends and behaviors that can be seen from the data. (Note: Here is the point where you need to understand how the different types of data can play a useful role.) The data segments that were identified were categorized and aligned into the following:

- Sentiment data—data from forums, emails, call center, websites and the Internet contains customer sentiments and provides useful insights into linking the customer sentiment and how it impacts the enterprise
- Behavioral data—data from sentiment can be used to create behavior analytics that will identify how individuals react to product issues and their influence across their network of friends and other connections
- Social graph data—data based on sentiment and behavior can be modeled into a social network graph using graph databases and visualization tools such as touchgraph
- Location data—geospatial data integrated with these data sets will help create heatmaps for how many clusters of product, population, and issues occur, how many solvers are available to solve the issues, and their geographic location. This data will be useful for both identifiable and anonymous customer situations
- Customer databases—internal customer databases that provide data about current customers and their products, support subscription, and such.

All of these data segments were combined into one layer using metadata integration and master data integration (as applicable). The overall expansion of data combined with the different models of analytics provides critical insights, which enabled the enterprise to understand how to create a strategic approach to understanding the customer in a nonpersonal interactive mode. The analytical models used included the following

- Classification models
  - Neural networks
  - Bayesian
- Clustering models
  - Canopy clustering
  - K-means clustering
  - Fuzzy K-means
  - Mean shift clustering
  - Hierarchical clustering
  - Top–down clustering
- Similarity algorithms
- Recommendation algorithms

The output from these computation models were visualized using mashup techniques to create an integrated perspective about a single user and a population cluster that has the same usage and behavior patterns. With the application of machine learning techniques together with these models and the data, an interactive process was established that could be integrated in websites, browsers, and channels where there is community of users and solvers. This paved the way for the enterprise to start participating in different touchpoints where their products were discussed and increased opportunities for them to connect with customers in an indirect channel, but providing valuable service that changes the customer perspective about the enterprise.

The actual implementation is a complex solution where the backend platforms performed the computations in real time in a distributed and parallel environment and the results were simulcast to call center, retail, and web channels. The overall transformation exercise was a 15-month implementation that directly resulted in a 40% lift in customer confidence (based on several independent surveys and customer sentiment on the Internet), more than 54% savings in spend on campaigns, a 34% recovery from revenue leakage.

All of this was possible from the data gathered across the social channels and further classifying them into the subcategories that created a vision for integration. The most important factor to understand here is the use of metadata and master data effectively to integrate the data from multiple channels irrespective of data quality.

This case study proves the value of the social data and how its use in collaborative computing changed the business interactions and resulted in profitability as expected.

Four Steps to Social Business Intelligence

CONTENTS

The world of data is abuzz with the tsunami called "Big Data." If you are a CXO this is a topic that will be haunting you at work, home, and even social gatherings. The biggest question that keeps nagging you is the business value from this mass of data called "big data." Take a step back for a moment and assess the same question with investments that has been made into a Sales-Force or Unica or Endeca implementation and the business value that you can derive from the same. Chances are you will not have an accurate picture of the amount of return on investment (ROI) or the percentage of impact in terms of increased revenue or decreased spend or process optimization percentages from any such prior experiences. Not that your teams did not measure the impact, but they are unsure of expressing the actual benefit into quantified metrics. But in the case of a big data implementation, there are techniques to establish a quantified measurement strategy and associate the overall program with such cost benefits and process optimizations.

The interesting question to ask is what are organizations doing with big data? Are they collecting it, studying it, working with it for advanced analytics? How exactly does the puzzle called big data fit into an organizations strategy and how does it enhance corporate decision-making?

To understand this picture better, there are some key questions that need to be answered.

1. How many days does it take on an average to get answers to the question "why"?
2. How many cycles of research does the organization do for understanding the market, competition, sales, employee performance, and customer satisfaction?
3. Can your organization create an executive blueprint along the Zachman framework model to provide you business answers on *who*, *what*, *where*, *when*, and *how*?
4. Do you believe that all the key insights are available and presented to the decision maker (executive or managerial) at the right time for the right context?
5. Do you believe that your workflow system can provide you metrics and indicators on key processes and their content?
6. Does your organization have data that teams can use to improve decisions, processes, and overall efficiencies but cannot process or use the same?
7. Do you have systems that are poor in metadata but are mission critical?
8. Do you have large volumes of data and have no idea of how to leverage the same?

There are more questions that one can come up with or ponder, but the key point that I'm driving in this process is to open your thoughts to look at the world through the eyes of data. There is an abundance of data that any organization has today and there is a lot of hidden data or information in these data nuggets that have to be harvested. Consider the following data

- Traditional business systems—enterprise resource planning (ERP), supply chain management (SCM), customer relationship management (CRM), sales force automation (SFA)
- Content management platforms
- Portals
- Websites
- Third-party agency data
- Data collected from social media
- Statistical data
- Research and competitive analysis data

- Point-of-sale data—retail or web channel
- Legal contracts
- Emails

If you observe a pattern here, there is data about customers, products, services, sentiments, competition, compliance, and much more available. The question is does the organization leverage all the data that is listed here? And more important is the question, Can you access all this data at relative ease and implement decisions? This is where big data comes into the picture, among the data nuggets that we have described, 50 percent or more are internal systems and data producers that have been used for gathering data but not harnessing analytical value (the data here is structured, semistructured, and unstructured), the other 50 percent or less is the new data that is called big data (web data, machine data, sensor data).

Social media and business intelligence integration will provide valuable insights into the external forces that influence and guide your business everyday.

The biggest question that puzzles the industry today is how to make this integration happen; there are a few distinct steps to take for creating this impact within your organization too, these are

STEP 1: CREATING AND ENGAGING SOCIAL MEDIA PRESENCE

Stage 1: Set up a Strategy and Goals to Accomplish

A very important step that gets skipped often—companies that succeed with social business intelligence achieve the same by setting up a strategy and goals that get accomplished with the set of strategies. This approach is the same and will provide success

- Whether you are looking to do social media to grow your business?
- Create awareness of your product or service?
- Or simply for customer service?

Many enterprises would like all the above, but if you focus on one area more than the others, it will help you to set your goals. Part of a strategy is also looking at your target market.

- Who's your audience?
- What are your goals?
- When do you want to achieve those goals?

Going into social media with a laser-targeted focus can make all the difference in the world on your results and outcomes.

Stage 2: Make a Plan and Content Calendar

Once your strategy is set up, now it is time to implement the plan. The simplest way is to be real organized and set up a content calendar. This calendar needs to consist of different types of posts. What types of content should you post? This depends on the social community that you want to create around your brand, products, and services. Apart from the creation, there is also participation in customer owned and driven content. You need to be able to foster the growth of both these channels simultaneously.

Stage 3: Post Your Content With Consistence

Once you have a schedule to post content, you need to schedule the content and track the changes consistently. To schedule, you can use tools like Hootsuite or the Facebook scheduler. Enterprises set up the post creation with one team, and this team collaborates the creation of the post and schedules the updates to happen. The ease of creating a team relives enterprises of the concern of recency of updates and the relevance of the data that is created. Another benefit from this approach is the ability to create some intense collaboration internally and externally in the organization.

Stage 4: Engage! Don't Just Post

This step is more important than any others, but also the most overlooked. Social media is not just about talking "at" people, it's about talking "to" people. To ensure success in your social media presence and create the visibility of participation in conversations, join in other conversations. The biggest success in the world of customers and prospects is to truly get to know and care about others and it will come back to you. Create a value system around the social media networks and avoid noise. This will create a true loyal set of folks that will benefit you and your brand in the short and long term.

Stage 5: Monitor What Works Best and Does Not Work

There are many tools that can help you in creating and monitoring your social media presence and participation. It is important to look at your statistics. There are many monitoring tools available, including Google Analytics, which is free; Facebook Insights; Twitter; and Instagram. You should be reviewing these weekly or biweekly at least. Sometimes, it takes some experimenting and really getting to know your audience for social media success.

Know what questions you need answered. Your monitoring tool can discover the who, what, where, when, and how of your audience's online behavior. Social listening can tell you who is posting what, where they are posting it, and how that fits in to the overall conversation, but first you need to supply the tool with a set of targeted keywords that will narrow down your search to find only the most relevant material. Think about the questions that you want answered in a broad sense and then translate that to search terms and exclusions that will do the trick.

STEP 2: TIE SOCIAL MEDIA MONITORING TO YOUR BUSINESS GOALS

You've identified your business goals as an enterprise. Now think about how social media analytics and business intelligence can help you achieve them. How will the answers help grow your business? This will also help you focus your questions. Social media analytics and social media metrics are not business metrics, so you will have to draw a connection between the nonfinancial and the financial. If you bake these connections into your online strategy, measuring the success later will be a hundred times easier.

STEP 3: DECIDE ON COLLABORATION

Decide what departments will use web and social media intelligence. Lots of people assume that marketing is the only department that can use social media insight. Not true. There are many more applications. Brand management is the most common, but you can also use social research to generate leads, learn competitive intelligence, do market/industry research, create a more efficient customer service model, discover a crisis and manage it, and run product/service research development. As more insight is gained and used in real-world situations, social media and online listening will become a core part of each department.

STEP 4: EXAMINE ANALYTICS FOR INSIGHTS

There's no need to obsess over every measurement that's out there. Look only at the metrics that matter. There will be some platform-specific metrics: likes, shares, followers, retweets, views, re-pins, etc. There are back-end measurements from your company website: page views, time spent on site, popular posts, keyword searches, conversion rates, etc. There's the more advanced web monitoring measurements that a listening tool offers: volume of mentions, sentiment activity, site types, top domains, top authors, most-used words, link spread, and influence measurement, etc. Then there are business metrics: total sales, new customers acquired, cost per transaction, number of qualified leads, number of customer service problems resolved, etc.

To verify the steps and stages and their impact, let's see the following case study.

CASE STUDY: CALL CENTER OPTIMIZATION

The worst fear of a customer is to deal with the call center. The fundamental frustration for the customer is the need to explain all the details about their transactions with the company they are calling, the current situation, and what they are expecting for a resolution, not once but many times (in most cases) to many people and maybe in more than one conversation. All of this frustration can be vented on their Facebook page or Twitter or a Social Media blog, causing multiple issues.

They will have an influence in their personal network that will cause potential attrition of prospects and customers.

Their frustration may be shared by many others and eventually result in class action lawsuits.

Their frustration will provide an opportunity for the competition to pursue and sway customers and prospects

All of these actions lead to one factor → ***revenue loss***

If this company continues to persist with poor quality of service, eventually the losses will be large and even lead to closure of business and loss of brand reputation. It is in situations like this where you can find a lot of knowledge in connecting the dots with data and create a powerful set of analytics to drive business transformation. Business transformation does not mean you need to change your operating model but rather it provides opportunities to create new service models created on data-driven decisions and analytics.

The company that we are discussing here, let us assume, decides that the current solution needs an overhaul and the customer needs to be provided the best quality of service, it will need to have the following types of data ready for analysis and usage.

Customer profile, lifetime value, transactional history, segmentation models, social profiles (if provided)

Customer sentiments, survey feedback, call center interactions

Product analytics

Competitive research

Contracts and agreements—customer specific

We can create or use metadata-driven architecture to integrate the data for creating these analytics. There is a nuance of selecting the right technology and architecture for the physical deployment.

A few days later, the customer calls for support, the call center agent is now having a mashup showing different types of analytics presented to them. The agent is able to ask the customer guided questions on the current call and apprise them of the solutions and timelines; rather than ask for information, they are providing a knowledge service. In this situation, the customer feels more privileged, and even if there are issues with the service or product, the customer will not likely attrite. Furthermore, the same customer now can share positive feedback and report their satisfaction, thus creating a potential opportunity for more revenue. The agent feels more empowered and can start having conversations on cross-sell and up-sell opportunities. In this situation, there is a likelihood of additional revenue and diminished opportunities for loss of revenue.

This is the type of business opportunities that social media data analytics (internal and external) will bring to the organization, along with steady improvement of efficiencies, creating optimizations and reducing risks and overall costs. There is some initial investment spend involved in creating this data strategy and architecture and implementing additional technology solutions. The ROI will offset these costs and even save on license costs from technologies that may be retired post the new solution. Social business intelligence is not a new generation of the insights but a game-changing Segway to analytics and insights when implemented, as strategy in organizations will cause a significant positive impact for the entire organization.

CASE STUDY: CREATING NEW MARKET OPPORTUNITIES

Summary

One of the leading publishers of scientific, technical, and medical information products and services, "Publisher XYZ," counts more than 2,500 journals and 23,000 books to its product portfolio. Overall, they serve nearly 30 million scientists, students, faculty, and health and science professionals worldwide. A global business headquartered in Amsterdam, the company employs 6,800+ people worldwide, and they have recently acquired technology publication giants across the United States and Europe to add more customer service portfolio to their bottom line.

As Publisher XYZ observed the Web's ability to connect customers with the research that matters most to them, the company began to expand its portfolio of online solutions by launching the largest abstract and citation database of peer-reviewed literature and quality web sources with smart tools to track, analyze, and visualize research, in 2004. As this area grew, they saw the opportunity to address additional challenges with regards to research performance, planning, and funding, and launched a suite of solutions and services in June 2009 to enable institutions around the world to better evaluate, establish, and execute research strategies.

Although it was a very exciting and innovative step for Publisher XYZ, there was a unique challenge in launching the suite: their sales and marketing teams were entering a new market. Traditionally serving the librarian community, new marketing strategies were required to go beyond the library and meet with institutional research leaders. They needed to quickly identify what worked—and what didn't—to drive new business opportunities from the suite. To help keep the sales and marketing teams connected in real time to the colleagues and information they needed to reach this new market, Publisher XYZ chose implementing an enterprise social software platform.

Challenge

■ New Market, New Challenges

When Publisher XYZ decided to build the product suite, the company wanted to move quickly to address the new market challenges and establish new revenue sources to diversify its digital services business. The net result was that the sales and marketing teams had little more than a half-year to prepare, leaving many uncertain and even anxious issues about how the company would evolve its skill sets to serve such a new market.

Internally, they realized that the current communication and collaboration mechanisms within sales, product, and marketing would further exacerbate the task if left unattended. Most sales collateral and marketing documents were sent via email, crowding inboxes and causing confusion about who had the most current information when they dialed into a meeting. The company intranet wasn't sufficient, either; like many corporate intranets, the organization required the assistance of IT to update it, allowing content to become stale or static.

Solution

■ *Easy, Secure Collaboration.*

With only months to form a sales and marketing strategy for the suite launch, Publisher XYZ wanted a collaboration offering that would provide minimalistic technical effort on the part of the company on the back end, while the solution would be easy and quick for employees to learn and derive value from quickly on the front end. Their end suite solution (Social Text) has extremely flexible software as a service (SaaS) model that resulted in gaining the benefits desired while delivering the acquisition and growth factor. The new deployment model of SaaS with a hosted solution offering reduced risk and issues for IT that would have made it complex to deploy the solution.

For the key stakeholders, the simplicity of enterprise social software applications made it easy for them to create and edit content in a way that hadn't been possible with the existing intranet. By the simple click of "edit" and "save," employees can modify content on a web page and easily share it with all their colleagues in real time using an enterprise micro blogging tool. They also utilized an enterprise social networking profiles tool from the same solution set where their sales, product, and marketing members could share expertise, project work, and other critical information with colleagues.

As more work migrates to the new platform for internal collaboration on sales and marketing, new research, new contributors, and more readers and users, to allow efficient processing of all information, a dedicated customer success manager (CSM) and their team have been constituted to ensure that people get the most business value from the platform.

Adding this type of solution does take time, and managing the outcomes is based on collaboration between the different players and their quest for success. In this situation, we have seen this happen over time with multiple rounds of success.

■ *New Go-To Resource for Sales, Product, and Marketing*

Prior to moving to a social media–like platform that provided the much needed success, the internal teams within sales, product, and marketing relied on email and the existing company intranet platforms to share information with each other about customers, market conditions, and collateral. But information inside of email boxes became "instantly outdated," and the intranet required IT assistance to do any heavy lifting of content. Both of these issues prevented successful collaboration within the company. In the first quarter of the new platform move, the foundational platform for collaboration was created to ensure that the most current data is always available for usage when the field teams are selling and updating information. Today, this collaboration platform is the most vital success factor to create, share, and collaborate on critical sales, product, and marketing information, including the following:

■ Product collateral
■ White papers

- Publicity and pricing sales tools
- Market feedback
- Competitive intelligence
- Presentation decks
- FAQs

To ensure that data updates and important information is always shared, there are internal emails and collaboration messages that are available to be sent with each data asset.

RESULTS

- Adapt Quickly, Improve Product Feedback, Beat Competitors

The benefits from sharing information openly inside the teams using a secure enterprise social software platform has been pervasive across both sales and marketing, and even product development. The sales and marketing teams are better in sync; they know having the most updated information as the market evolves is helping them with a "Blue Ocean" strategy and success. In the end state today every account manager knows he or she enters every meeting with the latest collateral, including market statistics and analytics, that helps them address customer needs and illustrate value.

On the marketing side, the volume of email decreased substantially, as marketing managers fielded fewer product questions and requests for collateral from sales and other stakeholders, with the collaboration suite providing answers that can be self-serviced with ease and success.

The knowledge being captured inside the suite by account managers and consultants out in the field has also helped improve product feedback and speed the time to which the development team can improve outcomes. The updates and upgrades to the software happen in weeks instead of months, by the implementation of agile iteration cycles of development and implementation

Now that product managers can read the additional stream of product feedback, they know what new features to prioritize. "In the past, product feedback that the sales and marketing team used to collect from customers would often take over a year to be implemented." Today the faster development cycle is so great for rapidly meeting the needs of our customers, and within the solution suite, the teams can easily share product feedback and the corresponding enhancements with each other.

It has also improved their ability to on-board new employees, who can see and learn from the content that has been edited and revised inside the solution suite. Because content today is tag-able and searchable, it has evolved to become institutional knowledge that transcends the tenure of any one employee. "The soft knowledge aspect is really important; today, the employees can see the progression of things. What did a slide deck look like a year ago compared to this year? Knowing these things gives us better context for what work we do out in the field." are the positive sentiments echoed by the managers within the enterprise.

CONCLUSION

The publishing industry and research community move quickly. By giving its people access to real-time information that's never stale or dated, Publisher XYZ gives its employees the best chance to win new customers and serve their current ones more effectively. As the market changes, so too will the content and resources that helps sales, product, and marketing professionals at Publisher XYZ adapt to the needs of their expanding market. All of this has been possible from the cross-departmental collaboration that has driven the improved customer satisfaction and opened up new opportunities that are essential in the customer-driven market of today, and which were not easy to solve in the past.

Valuable Data for the Enterprise

CONTENTS

The world of social media has generated data from consumers like never before. The virtual groundswell on any topic today can create tipping points that can impact an enterprise and its brand in the market. The insights that can be captured from social media data can be applied immediately to improve outcomes and can also be applied with latencies to adjust a phased change in the outcomes. In order to understand the insights, we need to understand the data and the contexts in which the data has been discussed and used in the organization. The benefits of these platforms are multiple in terms of how it can position and change the organization. Using these approaches in internal collaboration and research and development types of activities, call center applications and social CRM are all very valuable to both the employee and the customers along with the organization, brand, and markets.

UNDERSTANDING SOCIAL DATA TYPES

In the landscape of social media and social networking platforms available for use by enterprises to implement a social analytics in the enterprise, each of them offers a unique value proposition to its users and delivers a mixture of data that can be leveraged by companies to monitor brand, enhance customer service, impact sales, or otherwise drive social data–fueled initiatives. Each social platform stores and produces a vast amount of information. Community members generate much of this data by authoring content and interacting with various features of the platform; the balance is generated by the systems themselves.[1] Facebook presently stores more than 100 petabytes of data dedicated specifically to the photo and video content produced and shared on the platform by its members.

Understanding the different data types available through these platforms is critical to building and designing analytic applications that impact enterprise companies. Social data can be classified into five categories

1. Behavioral data
2. Sentiment data
3. Social network data
4. Location / geographic data
5. Rich media data

Once we create a clear classification of the different types of data, we can work on integrating the data with other enterprise data assets to build a robust data platform for use with analytical platforms and data mining exercises. Let us examine each type of data and some examples of how the data has been used today in the industry.

Behavioral Data

Behavior data can be described as a transactional view of how an individual or group interacts on a social platform or across a network of business platforms. As we read through the exchanges that happen in these closed and open networks, we quickly realize how a pattern of thought exchanges between people from different locations, culture, and socioeconomic backgrounds influence their rationale and change outcomes in many situations. When a groundswell based on several of these types of exchanges and outcomes occur, we reach a tipping point and quickly see the impact on the end result. One noteworthy point here is that the entire series of exchanges, outcomes, and groundswell happens in hours and days not weeks and months. An excellent example of how behavioral data can provide a company with deep insight into its customer base is the success that the Target Corporation has had with its pregnancy prediction model. A program developed by Andrew Pole, group manager, Guest Marketing Analytics, to drive sales for existing customers whose behavior indicated they may be pregnant. In his article "How Companies Learn Your Secrets,"[2] *New York Times* reporter Charles Duhigg details how Target created analytic models based on purchase history, third-party data, basket analysis, website interactions, and

---

[1] Facebook Newsroom. Engineering and infrastructure [cited 2012 Feb 12]. Available from: URL: http://newsroom.fb.com/content/default.aspx?NewsAreaId=138
[2] Duhigg C. How companies learn your secrets. New York Times 2012 Feb 16 [cited 2012 Mar 3]. Available from: URL: http://www.nytimes.com/2012/02/19/magazine/shopping-habits.html

demographic data to determine the likelihood of a Target customer being pregnant in order to deliver highly focused and timely sales offers. Because Target assigns each of its customers a unique Guest ID, they are able to track and analyze the customer's behavior across many platforms over time. Pole began his analysis with the companies' baby registry database and determined how shopping behavior evolved once a customer signed up for the registry. He identified a pool of 25 critical products that when purchased in certain combinations could identify when a customer was pregnant and approximately how far along they were in the process. After using the registry data as an analytic model proving ground, Pole applied the program to the entire Target guest database and immediately identified thousands of customers who were likely pregnant. This behavioral analysis allows Target to deliver advertising and offers to these customers and helped the company realize greater revenue through the program. Target leverages its custom ad delivery system to merge the pregnancy offers into its normal flow of offers for these guests, so they appear to be there without the customer having insight into the work that took place to identify their condition.

Not all behavioral data is as well defined as the Target Corporation scenario, a less sophisticated example is the process by which advertising networks use behavioral data to determine the "next best offer." When a community member on a social platform posts that they have a cold, it's common for the platform to analyze the unstructured text content of their post and serve a marketing offer from a company that specializes in cold medicine remedies. The act of visiting a highly targeted web community can trigger the same effect. The theme or content focus of a social platform can trigger other sites in that network to offer content-centric marketing. I recently did some research online for a gnocchi roller; it's a device that puts the ridges in gnocchi-style pasta. I located one I liked at the William Sonoma website and for a week afterwards an ad for Williams and Sonoma followed me around the Internet. The only way this could have been executed was if the original site shared my behavioral data with a network of other sites. I'm confident that nothing personal was shared but it was clear that a session variable or cookie had been placed in my browser allowing the other sites to "recognize" me as I entered their platform. Retailers run a small risk of creeping their customers out with this type of targeted interaction, but in the end most people don't notice or are not technically savvy enough to determine its origins.

5.1 INTERNET COOKIE

An Internet cookie is a simple text string that a web server passes to your Internet browser. The information in the cookie allows the site to identify your browser when it visits the site. Many sites use cookie technology to deliver content or ads that align with your interests or past behavior. Cookies are not dangerous but they do allow a website to track and store information about your interactions. Some websites share your data in an anonymized fashion so their partners can track and learn your behaviors as you move between sites.

Behavioral data is often multistructured or polystructured in its form, making it difficult to leverage in traditional data management systems. The identity and transparency of behavioral data varies greatly by source. In the Target example, they were able to match up the behaviors with master records of the customer; they're Guest ID's. In many cases, social platforms will deidentify the individual's data to address privacy policies. This is why many enterprise companies are focused on aligning their business applications, websites, CRM systems, and customer contact points so they can organize customer data into a unified view that allows for greater utilization of this type of data from customers and prospects.

Analytics from Behavior data can be argued as skewed from a statistical analysis perspective. The reason for this argument is that a tipping point can influence the behavior of a crowd and when that trigger occurs, the data set can have several new outliers that were good prospects or customers in the model originally. Sometimes this model of analysis results in companies mistiming their offers or oversubscribing their customers with multiple conflicting offers in a shorter duration. One of the best techniques to reduce risk is to create a machine-learning model that can use several training sets of actual customer or prospect data along with behavioral data using geospatial integration to match population segments. These training sets can be simulated to create several scenarios, and the model can be adjusted to monitor and manage the outcomes in a positive result. The model once completed for desired outcomes can be optimized many times and even cloned and redefined to suit the company's need.

Behavior data can also be used to study cluster behaviors for populations by geography, demography, and socioeconomic factors. The data set available is so rich in geospatial information that we can gather how a person's sharing of intent and interest from one geographic region of the world can influence trends and followers in another geography. For example, viral videos of human rights protest is one good example where there was a global uprising in the social media supporting the cause. Similarly, a disaster readiness program can help people to be alert when natural calamities occur. By studying population segments and affinity behaviors, insurance companies can reduce risk of variable claims, health agencies can prevent or minimize disease outbreak, and much more.

Another good example of behavior data usage can be seen from social media-savvy enterprises. Kraft Foods is a great example where the company established a community portal called "Kraft Collaboration Kitchen" (http://www.kfcollaborationkitchen.com). Consumers are invited to submit solutions in the form of recipes at the portal, where Kraft has a set of outlined problems that need a solution or simply share a recipe on the community portal. Kraft uses a peer-driven gamification model to rank the recipe, and the winner is the most voted submission. Apart from the gamification implementation, there can be several technologies and statistical models used in creating the underlying platform, including search appliances, sentiment analytics, statistical algorithms, databases, and extended big data platforms. The community side of the portal is all about the members and what they are sharing and talking about. With an open innovation driven by community portals and focus, Kraft can use behavior modeling techniques and infer tremendous insights on the market pulse about what is trending and new, what are customers saying about them and the competition, and what kinds of marketing campaign have the most positive effect on their customers and across markets. They can also study the behavior of different geographies and compare and contrast behaviors of population segments within the geography.

As we see from these examples, behavior data has some extremely useful insights that can help optimize any organization's goals for customer-centric business models and open innovation. Not only can you understand the pulse of the customer, you can also predict the behavior and the associated outcome with better confidence.

Sentiment Data

At its core, sentiment data refers to the positive and negative opinions, ratings, recommendations, conversations, images, and videos that can be found on social platforms and within business application data. Sentiment data is considered to be the most valuable data set on the social web.

Understanding what customers or the community feel about your brand, products, or service is directly connected to revenue, foot traffic, and web traffic and today ranks as the first place companies look to when incorporating social data into their analytic strategy.

Social recommendation data is highly valuable when applied with clustering and regression algorithms. The most common trend that any basic analytical process has shown is that most consumers would follow the recommendation of a friend or a group of peers over a brand or marketing message. Understanding who acts as a promoter of your brand and who doesn't can be a valuable data point within any company that's smart enough to listen to and analyze the information. But that trend is not the only analytic that enterprises care about from sentiment data. The other trends that are useful include

- Context of the sentiment
- Reasons for the sentiment—whether a process failed in the interaction (e.g., too long lines or too much wait on the telephone) or the product or service simply failed to meet expectations

- Location of the event
- Strength of the tone
- Number of followers and influence
- Number of posts and reposts
- Geographic concentration
- Time period of activity

From a simple post, we can gain all this insight by exploring the data effectively. As an example, consider a tweet like this:

> @united #fail on wifi in redcarpet clubs (tooslow), delayedflight, customer service in redcarpet club lousy. Why fly u?

A simple analysis from this statement can get the following

- Context of the sentiment—Poor service in Red Carpet Club
- Inference—Important loyal customer
- Reasons for the sentiment—No return favor as promised for loyalty club and frequent fliers in airport locations
- Location of the event—airport and red carpet club
- Strength of the tone—Negative

And further analysis will yield the other attributes that we could discover from the example. The usefulness of this type of analysis will yield deeper information about the sentiment and its underlying cause. This is critical to understand, as the person or group that starts the thread is the biggest influencer in this chain and the person or groups that contribute most conversation become the population cluster that will be modeled for the overall sentiment and associated actions.

An international coffee company utilized sentiment data and integrated it with an analytic system, to monitor a product launch in real time. Prior to launching a new flavored coffee, the company connected to social sentiment data sources that included coffee lover blogs, Twitter, and niche coffee discussion forums from where they collected raw data about coffee as it was being discussed in the forums. The social sentiment data thus collected was combined with an advanced analytics platform that parsed the unstructured information in the blogs and forums as it was produced and were able to create greater insight by determining age, gender, preferences, sentiments, personalized comments, and regions of the customers based on advanced text analytics. This data set was used as the training set for a machine-learning model that was the live system on the day of the launch.

As the product launch day arrived, the company was able to use the analytical model and scan streaming data collected from "listening posts" in real time and quickly identify a negative price sensitivity trend as well as a flavor strength objection, which are considered as key metrics by the company. Using traditional data, they would have had to wait for sales trends to form over a much longer period of time or spend the money and resources required for infield market surveys and may still have been in the dark concerning the two critical trends that the social data analysis identified immediately.

5.2 LISTENING POST

A listening post is a data collection point and can be executed as real-time back end listeners that collect data from websites or static listeners implemented as surveys, forms, and other data collection techniques.

The coffee company was able to make fast pricing decisions and provide first-person commentary to their manufacturing R&D teams concerning taste based on the market response. The flavor issue with the product would normally have been exposed after many time-consuming and costly customer focus groups coupled with slow sales and loss of campaign revenue. Collecting data through in-store surveys and other data-gathering techniques, the company would have been challenged to tap such a widely disbursed set of customers or as many opinions using that format.

The coffee company was able to identify the wants and needs of their customer base without being intrusive, by asking for micro-surveys and website interactions and chat logs. In a very short window, they modified the flavor profile to meet the feedback they had received and executed a pricing strategy that was regionally based to overcome the issue. The company experienced significant success with the launch and gave credit to the ability to listen to sentiment data in real time from sources that were informed and influential to their business.

Social Graph Data

Social graph data represents one of the most sophisticated data sources in the social sphere. It is the network representation of a social platform members' direct and indirect social links—the "who you know and how you know them in a graph" (Figure 5.1).

In 2011, Facebook released research[3] that illustrates just how important our social graphs are becoming. In the research post, Facebook challenged the idea of "six degrees of separation," the premise that any two people are separated by no more than six connections. Hungarian author Frigyes Karinthy put forth

---

[3] Backstrom L. Anatomy of Facebook. Facebook Data Blog 2011 Nov 21 [cited 2012 Jan 14]. Available from: URL: http://www.facebook.com/notes/facebook-data-team/anatomy-of-facebook/10150388519243859

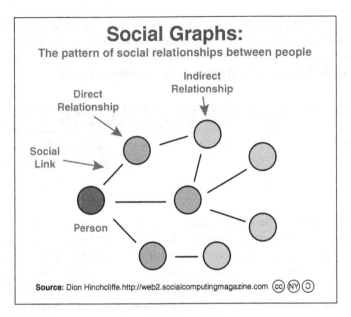

FIGURE 5.1 Social graph data—a web of relationships and influence

the original hypothesis in 1929. Facebook worked with the Laboratory for Web Algorithmics of the "Università degli Studi di Milano" to analyze the nearly 721 million[4] Facebook users in its member database and determined that the world is now closer than Mr. Karinthy thought. The average distance of separation in 2008 was 5.28 hops, and in 2011 it was 4.74. In the end, we are all more closely related than we thought and these relationships can tell an awful lot about us.

By analyzing an individual's social graph, a view of a person's interests and interactions can be created, additional value can be added to this analysis if information is already known about others in the graph and can be integrated with the view of the primary individual. A simple use case example is how credit card companies have included social graph analysis in their fraud and risk management algorithms. One firm gives positive weight to the algorithm if a prospect has a LinkedIn account, and additional significance is given based on how old the profile is. If their profile data aligns with information the credit card company has on file, it adds more positive weight. The company then analyses the job titles of the credit applicant's social graph and provides a score based on how many executive-level connections are in their sphere of

---

[4] Backstrom L, Boldi P, Rosa M, Ugander J, Vigna S. Four degrees of separation. Cornell University Library—Computing Research Repository 2012 Jan 6 [cited 2012 Feb 11]. Available from: URL: http://arxiv.org/abs/1111.4570

influence. The assumption for the credit card firm is simple: if you have a profile that's been online for a couple of years and it accurately matches data they have on file and your social circle is predominantly white color/executive level, they believe you're statistically less likely to commit fraud or default on your credit card or loan. It's obvious that privacy issue will play a role in how we use social data and this example stands out on that subject. We'll cover privacy in a later chapter.

One of the most commonly used behavior analytics from social graphs is predicting customer churn in enterprises, especially wireless telecommunications and set-top box provider space. As an example, let us say John Doe is a customer of wireless carrier XYZ corp. He is very frustrated with the level of service and quality of calls, the lack of smartphones at affordable prices, and the lack of an unlimited everything calling plan. In this situation, he runs across an advertisement from a competitor who is mass commoditizing the wireless service spectrum and offers a no-contract plan that offers the best features and can save him almost 30 percent off his monthly bills. John Doe decides that he has had enough with his current provider and switches to the new carrier. He is very pleased with the long-term savings and the overall service, and he updates his social media profiles with his experience, including the old and the new experience. At this point, John is sharing his sentiment and opinions to a network of friends. A social graph plot will provide insights into how many of his friends are having a closely knit relationship where they will potentially leave the wireless carrier if they are having the same service provider. The social graph will provide insights into the degree of relationship, which can be used to compute the level of potential attrition.

Another example of social graphs is using common interests and topics to create a connected network. The primary node of this graph is the most influential person and the rest of the graph connects the remaining members to this topic and person by the weight of the relationship, which can be multidimensional attributes applied to the topic in general. The bottom line with the social graph is the ability to classify groups of individuals based on location, topic, and influence. By creating various graphs and analyzing the nodes as a two-dimensional object, companies can analyze their customer and their social circle of relationships, the people whom they influence and the people who influence them, the topics they influence and the topics that influence them. A large fast food company used social graphs to connect customer behavior on sunny days versus rainy days for drive-through purchase of the same type of food and beverage. Using the data from social graphs, the company was able to predict how much sales of a product can happen in a given day and, using that data, they were able to plan labor utilization and optimize supply-chain models. There are many such leverage points that can be derived from the model when applied with the right analytics.

LOCATION/GEOGRAPHIC DATA

Location/geographic data is produced by social platform members as well as the devices they use to interact with the platform. The data is generally well structured and in many cases delivers latitude (Lat) and longitude (Long) data available for analysis. The growth of mobile computing devices and growing functionality of smartphones are causing geographic data to stream into social platforms at an astounding rate. Social location data is often available in conjunction with behavioral data as well as sentiment data. The combination of these three valuable data types in one place is irresistible to enterprise companies.

Marketers were early adopters of social location data and have quickly integrated this data type into targeted campaigns. A common use case is custom delivering advertising based on location, when using a social check-in service such as FourSquare, a community member alerts the application that they are in a certain location, the application can then serve an offer that's nearby and fits your past behavioral profile, that is, offering a 30 percent–off coupon to your favorite type of restaurant while avoiding the chain you recently shared negative sentiment about online or your favorite hotel chain sending an email offer after you post your vacation plans for San Francisco. These are straightforward cases merging social location data into marketing campaigns and they will generally have a higher success rate based on being contextually and geographically accurate.

A good example of combining location-based intelligence and behavior data is promotion of products and services based on search patterns. For example, consider that you are walking along Pier 39 in San Francisco on a chilly day and you are searching for food nearby to your location. After you search for restaurants, you get a promotional message that a local coffee shop is offering a combo of chocolate and coffee for $3.99 that day, chances are, depending on the time, you may walk over to the coffee chop rather than search for a restaurant. This trend is called "personalization of services" in the industry and it is the most effective technique to influence a customer to purchase a product or service with your offer.

Progressive companies have found ways to integrate social location data with enterprise applications and processes such as supply chain analytics helping to drive revenue and more effective inventory management. A leading electronics firm is integrating a combination of social location data and social signal from Twitter into their supply chain algorithms. They utilize the Lat/Long data included in Twitter feeds to focus only on the social signal within a small radius of each of their retail locations. As they monitor, they filter the information to listening for content that indicates buying trends centric to brands or types of electronics. They analyze the information and includes it in their algorithms, adding the data to decision processes on stock mix and levels. This nonintrusive "market monitoring" is sophisticated and can add a few percentage points of accuracy to supply chain management models.

Personalization of services includes marketing, micro-targeting, and location-based offers. These nonintrusive techniques have created a positive impact on the customer, for companies that have engaged in this model of customer-centric transformation. An unspoken benefit from this type of service is the trigger of behaviors of sharing the experience using social channels, word-of-mouth marketing, and increase in loyalty. Along with these benefits, companies can also realize what search patterns occur in a Lat-Long area in a given region or zip code. They can apply that to a larger population or compare similar economic backgrounds of lat–long and study behaviors of searches. The list of possibilities is endless once you have the basic architecture and data collection mechanism in place.

RICH MEDIA DATA

Rich media data represents video, audio, and photographic content produced and shared on social platforms. Attached to the media content is a highly useful layer of metadata information that can be leveraged for analytic insight. These media assets are generally wrapped in information such as creator name and profile data, titles, abstracts, rankings, keywords, geographic locations, device information, date authored, and social member commentary. These data attributes are features associated with the rich data artifact that can be extracted to be analyzed along with other data sets to harness greater insights.

Analyzing the rich data is a complex process. As it stands today, we have two processing approaches for rich media data:

- Images and static pictures are processed using feature extraction algorithms and techniques, where we extract the critical pieces of image data and run statistical analysis. This is a limited exercise in the industry and is not applied in daily analysis yet.
- Videos and audio—For audio, we convert speech to text and use the output to perform analysis. Videos are processed in two steps, first the audio is extracted and tagged with the metadata and then the audio is processed to text, where the metadata is applied and the final result is processed as text mining data sets.

In the current state, we do the following processing steps with rich media data:

- Acquire the data
- Tag the data with vital metadata
- Classify the data

- Categorize the data
- Collect the metadata and store the same
- Process the data applying one of the techniques discussed earlier in this section
- Store the outputs for analysis as required

Because of the complex nature of this process, we have limited the data from this type of social media data to tagging and metadata collections.

An example is the social restaurant review site Yelp, where members share photographs, location, and sentiment data about different restaurants, their rating of the ambience, food, service, and much more, based on their experience. While restaurants potentially collect data from Yelp or other aggregators, they might not focus on the content classified as rich media data, looking only at the text and in the process miss the context of the entire thread of discussion, which might be a picture or a video or a report or a search result set.

Rich media has a great capacity to effect brands and reputation online. An excellent example is the *United Breaks Guitars* video posted to YouTube on July 6, 2009 (Figure 5.2). Since its premier, more than 11,736,000 people have watched the video that claimed United Airlines was responsible for breaking the guitar of Juno Award–winning recording artist Dave Carroll. Mr. Carrroll created a music video to chronicle his customer service experiences with the airline as he attempted to get reimbursed for the damaged instrument. After months of working with United, they were unable to come to terms over the issue and Mr. Carroll released the video to air his frustration. In a matter of days, it went viral and was replayed on most every major news program on television as well as most late night programs. United failed to see how fast the issue was growing online and replied to inquires with a rather static customer service response. In the end, the damage done to United's reputation was extremely significant and Mr. Carroll had become a bit of a folk hero.

The video has received more than nearly 30,000 community member comments and more than 56,000 "likes." If United had been listening to the rich media social signal, they would have seen the 24+ mentions of their brand on the video page and could have quickly analyzed the sentiment of the comments to determine the depth of this public relations failure and acted with a strategy. Instead, they fumbled the ball and ended up looking nothing short of inept. I urge you watch the video; it can be found at http://www.youtube.com/watch?v=5YGc4zOqozo. The moral of the story is, ignoring a public statement and backlash by maintaining silence does not help your brand. Had United been more diligent about the issue and accepted the breakdown in service or used the incident to improve the baggage-handling process or issue a policy that fragile equipment as baggage will need an extra cost, it might have made its reputation better. Recently, Mr. Carroll has announced he is starting a new

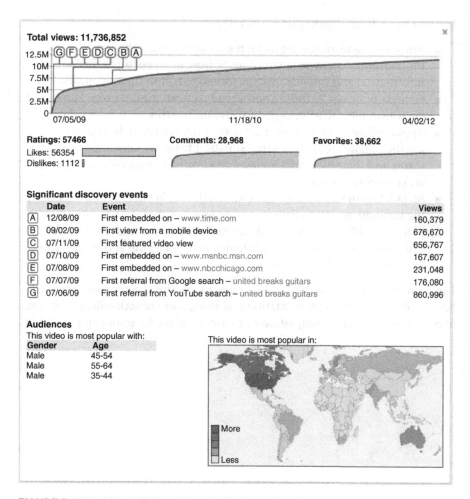

Total views: 11,736,852

Significant discovery events		
Date	**Event**	**Views**
A	12/08/09	First embedded on – www.time.com	160,379
B	09/02/09	First view from a mobile device	676,670
C	07/11/09	First featured video view	656,767
D	07/10/09	First embedded on – www.msnbc.msn.com	167,607
E	07/08/09	First embedded on – www.nbcchicago.com	231,048
F	07/07/09	First referral from Google search – united breaks guitars	176,080
G	07/06/09	First referral from YouTube search – united breaks guitars	860,996

FIGURE 5.2 United Breaks Guitars—Dave Caroll's Journey Turned Upside Down. The Statistics Video is from Youtube.

business focused on helping corporations better understand the impact of social media on customer service.

As mentioned at the beginning of the chapter, there are hundreds of social media platforms, each producing a mix of the five social data types—sentiment, behavioral, social graph, location, and rich media. Each offers compelling insights into customers, clients, and members of social communities. Like any other source of data, social media has lots of data and all types of data as applied by its users. Organizations need to understand the category of data and how to access the same, what values to derive from that data set, and how to incorporate it into their workflow and business measurement process.

Key takeaways from the chapter are as follows:

- Integrating and analyzing social media data creates challenges for traditional analytic environments: how to access this valuable information and provide insights for usage within the organization.
- Context of data—Without appropriate context, the data seen is more of noise and rubbish as opposed to relevant insights.
- Applicability of data—Using the correct data in the right context is another challenge. This is a true situation between sales and marketing teams and their use of data related to areas like campaign management and customer interaction.
- Metadata—In terms of integration, it will be a key focus area, especially the business metadata integration. In terms of creating an internal platform with the integrated data sets from outside and inside, extending taxonomies and ontologies as data tagging and exploratory frameworks will be very useful.

There are several case studies and discussions in the chapters further in the book to illustrate the implementation and integration of technology solutions to complete the internal adaptation from the social media solution framework.

Accessing the Data

CONTENTS

The biggest challenge in the world of social media data is the data itself, which has a mix of noise and value as one angle of the triangle, privacy and compliance issues as the second angle, and the third angle is the technology and process needed to harness the data. Why should we understand these problems before we build a platform and how do companies need to build a structured organization around the entire program are all questions that will come to your mind at this point? This chapter will address the data accessibility and infrastructure architectures for social media data, and chapters following this will address governance, structure, and other details.

A simple process flow for understanding the social media data collection process is shown in Figure 6.1.

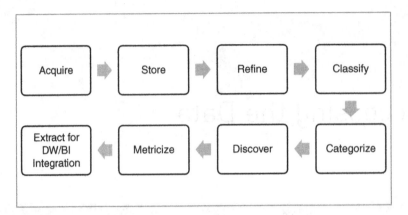

FIGURE 6.1 Social media data collection process—Concept

There are seven steps that need to be accomplished for collecting data from social media sources, prior to integrating the same with data from the data warehouse as seen from the picture in Figure 6.1. Each of these processes can be executed as a set of processes with cycles of data and information that will be processed through.

ACQUIRE

The first step in integrating and processing data from social media sources is acquisition of data. There are three substeps in this process, as described in Figure 6.2, namely, monitor, collect, and store.

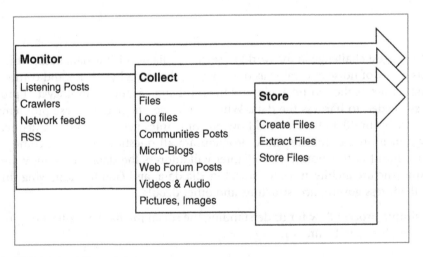

FIGURE 6.2 Acquisition technique concept

Before we discuss the details of the acquisition process, social media data can be harnessed directly by an organization with its own processes or purchased from a third-party data aggregator like GNIP or DataSift. There are significant differences in the two approaches that can radically alter the course of information management within any organization. If the company is buying the data as third-party source from GNIP or DataSift as the standard package, the format of the data, structure, and output will be defined by these organizations and the data will be dropped as files ready for extraction. Any additional details needed for the tweets, Facebook posts, or any website shares will need to be procured separately and then processed as additional feeds. The plus point in this format feed is the readiness of the product to be packaged and executed in hours from the time a contract is signed on. On the other hand, you can also set up your own data acquisition layer to extract data from the unstructured side of the data world. This will require any organization to go through the following steps, and once these steps are set up correctly, the enterprise can repeat the steps to capture data on demand as needed. However, the format of the data captured will need to be managed, as changes will still need to be captured and defined within the scope of the program. Additional cycles of work will be needed at any point when a change is added to the process whether it is to add or remove data elements. The steps that need to be implemented are discussed in the next sections.

- Monitor

  To process data from social media, we need to adopt a different approach than collecting transactional data, which originates from a database-driven architecture. This approach is called as the "monitor" phase, where we will closely listen to chatter on social media about topics of interest concerning the brand, reputation, services, experience, and peer rating, among others. There are several techniques applied today to monitoring information from social media. The most popular themes are as follows:

  - Listening Posts—One of the best data collection efforts today is by implementing listening posts. From a basic definition perspective, the rise of the "social media listening post," a new breed of system designed to plug directly into social networks and constantly watching for feedback automatically around the clock about the brand, competition, market, and consumer satisfaction.

    In today's market- and consumer-driven situation, many future thinking companies have already taken steps toward building such systems. How do you keep track right now? Without understanding the market and the consumer that drives it, how can you make decisions about your direction and next steps? In the past (read this with less than 10 years as the past), any business would normally engage third-party providers for surveys or focus groups to conduct surveys and collect response from groups of consumers, who would take time to participate in such an activity. In that time, your brand could have been suffering ongoing damage, and by the time you find out, valuable customers have been lost.

Intelligence is readily available these days on a near-instantaneous basis, can we afford not to use it? This is the biggest question that gets raised today in enterprises by executives and budget owners. The rapid advancement in technology over the last few years (specially between 2000 and 2008) provides us with a rich selection of platforms that can process structured and unstructured data together and provide the end user with a rich mashup of data about them, their competition, and the overall market. However the skills needed to perform this kind of analysis is still a growing area, and this is where many organizations feel the struggle when they are implementing a listening post or a social media integration program. From discussions with teams that have been implementing these platforms over the last decade, the areas that are consistently challenging are

- Complexity of data integration—e.g., unstructured, semistructured, evolving schema etc
- Complexity of analysis—e.g., determining sentiment: is it really a positive or negative statement with respect to the brand?
- Complexity of data volume—to gain a complete picture of public opinion toward your brand or organization through social media, many millions of web sites and data services must be consumed, continuously around the clock. They need to be analyzed in complex ways, far beyond traditional data warehouse query functionality.
- Complexity of data visualization—to gain the best understanding of what is happening with your brand in the social media spectrum, you need to visualize the data that you have collected, and herein is the complexity of the grain of data and the semantic integration challenges with the metadata layer of data.

The availability or accessibility of the data is one kind of complexity to deal with in terms of volume of the data and the velocity, the other challenge that lies in this aspect is the format of the data available. Data format varies greatly among social media sources, ranging from regular "structured" data through semi- and unstructured forms, to complex polystructured data with many dimensions. This structural complexity poses extreme difficulty for traditional data warehouses and upfront ETL (extract–transform–load) approaches, and demands a far more flexible data consumption platform that can digest the data in the format and structure that it originates from. Let us take a couple of examples at this point to understand this

- Facebook data—The data source feeds from Facebook can be extracted into structured or polystructured outputs using the API. The issue in the data lies in the fact that data is associated with users of the system and the user can have different subjects of interest and have different communities of relationships based on the topic of discussion. When you extract the data from a user, not only is the subject matter of the content important but the context of the subject is very important too, as it will provide a layer of abstraction for semantic data integration purposes.
- Forum data—On the other hand, if you extract data from web forums, this data has similar complexities to the data from Facebook but is simple enough from the perspective of what you want to access in the fact that the conversations happening are focused on specific subjects and topics, which make it easier from the extraction and semantic integration perspective. There are complexities like the level of user, the knowledge of the conversational topic, and the depth of experience, and extracting these definitions and associated metrics are not simple but the format of the data is semistructured.
- Document data—A third kind of format is the document format where the language and the context of each sentence will be processed and extracted for creation of metrics and associated subjects. The processing of this type of data needs multiple types of business rules to be applied to the document to gain the appropriate context and the meaning of the document.

The biggest question that needs an answer is how do we architect a system that can process data like this in a common platform? The complexity increases as you start looking at accessing data from all the different systems in an organization that are used to create decision support platforms. The overall requirements need distributed data analysis and processing.

Big data platforms from the Internet company perspective have been designed to address problems where you have volume, variety, or velocity of data with the complexity and ambiguity associated with the semantic frameworks and the resulting analytical outcomes. Every use-case from a business strategy and architecture viewpoint look toward the cutting edge of the technology, and look for a platform that supports near-real-time, streaming data capture and analysis, with the capability to implement Machine Learning algorithms for the analytics/sentiment analysis component.

For the back end, a high-throughput data capture/store/query capability is required, suitable for continuous streaming operation, probably with redundancy/high-availability, and a nonrigid schema layer capable of evolving over time as the data sources evolve. So-called No-SQL database systems (which in fact stands for "not only SQL" rather than "no SQL") such as Cassandra, HBase, or MongoDB offer excellent properties for high-volume streaming operation, and would be well suited to the challenge, or there are also commercial derivatives of some of these platforms on the market, such as the excellent Acunu Data Platform that commercializes Cassandra. Additionally, a facility for complex analytics, most likely via parallel, shared-nothing computation (due to the extreme data volumes) will be required to derive any useful insight from the data you capture. For this component, paradigms like MapReduce are a natural choice, offering the benefits of linear scalability and unlimited flexibility in implementing custom algorithms, and libraries of machine learning such as the great Apache Mahout project have grown up around providing a toolbox of analytics on top of the MapReduce programming model. Hadoop is an obvious choice when it comes to exploiting the MapReduce model, but since the objective here is to achieve near-real-time streaming capability, it may not always be the best choice. Cassandra and HBase (which in fact runs on Hadoop) can be a good choice since they offer the low-latency characteristics, coupled with MapReduce analytic capabilities.

Finally, some form of front-end visualization/analysis layer will be necessary to graph and present results in a usable visual form. There are some new open-source business intelligence (BI) analytics tools around that might do the job, or a variety of commercial offerings in this area. The exact package to be selected for this component is strongly dependent on the desired insight and form of visualization and so is probably beyond the scope of this article, but of course requirements are clear that it needs to interface with whatever back-end storage layer you choose.

Given the cutting-edge nature of many of the systems required, a solid operational team is really essential to maintain and tune the system for continuous operation. Many of these products have complex tuning requirements demanding specialist skill with dedicated headcount. Some of the commercial open-source offerings have support packages that can help mitigate this requirement, but either way, the need for operational resource must never be ignored if the project is to be a success.

The technologies highlighted here are evolving rapidly, with variants or entirely new products appearing frequently, as such it would not be unreasonable to expect significant advancement in this field within the 6- to 12-month time frame. This will likely translate into advancement on two fronts: increased and functional capability of the leading distributed data platforms in areas such as query interface and indexing capability, and reduced operational complexity and maintenance requirements.

- Crawlers—Accessing data requires collection of the data from sources and processing to integrate them into a common platform where they are accessed, processed, and brought into an analytical engine for creating the analytics required to integrate them with structured data systems. Internet search engines gave us the ability to think about using crawlers for the purpose of listening to data elements in the web and accessing them for analysis and integration. The crawlers need to perform the following operations
  - Listening—waiting on the Internet to listen to the discussions about the brand and scraping the details of the discussions.
  - Collect—categorizing the discussions and adding context to the topic, channel, date, and overall length of the discussions.
  - Store—create file outcomes that can be stored in the platform for further analysis, discovery, and integration.
- Store

Storage of data collected from the social media occurs in different aspects and the program control for each aspect will differ from the other. There are two types of data collection—listener based and third-party based. The listener-based collection technique will revolve around the listening and collection of data, which will be accrued as files and stored into the system. These files need to be named, classified, and categorized with the appropriate tags for preprocessing and semantic integration.

The third-party data access is a contract that is executed with a company that will access data and create a file/files, which will be delivered to a landing zone or ftp server. These files will be named per source to enable the identification of the files and their data format. They are then classified and categorized for preprocessing and integration purposes.

In a processing architecture, the classic flow is shown in Figure 6.3. The files are processed with a metadata engine (HCatalog in Hadoop and Metastores in NoSQL databases) upon acquisition to assign the right format and structure to the file. The process is under the store data flow after the data is landed in the landing zone.

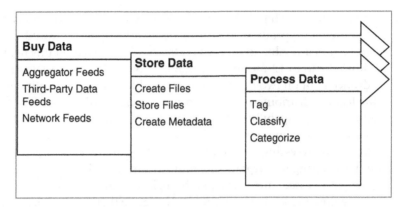

FIGURE 6.3 Processing Technique Concept

REFINE

The next set of processing data after the storage is the refinement of the data. There are four steps in the process as shown in Figure 6.4.

- Filter—In this step, we create business rules to process the data collected and classified. The two basic rules are to remove noisy data and remove incomplete data. This process, while needing parallel execution to complete in a short time frame, creates a data set that is complete and valid; the workload for removing incomplete data is simple but the removal of noisy data is time consuming and requires several iterations of processing.

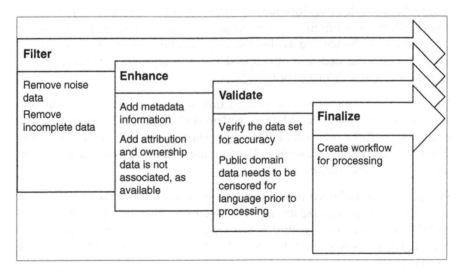

FIGURE 6.4 Refine process concept

- Enhance—In this step, we enhance the data set from the filter stage by adding the appropriate semantic metadata to process the data for integration and discovery purposes. In the enhancement process, we also cover the data stewardship areas of ownership and audit controls.
- Validate—In this step, we validate the data set for its accuracy and readiness for processing. Special care for language and processing will be applied for textual data in this step. Any legal concerns need to be addressed in this step.
- Finalize—In this step, we will create the workflow for data integration and discovery processing to be applied to the data.

CLASSIFY

As data sets are ready for processing, we apply the next step called as classify, shown in Figure 6.5. In this step, the data is tagged based on the metadata and we create the external linkage to the source and internal linkage to the enterprise metadata. Once we complete these steps, we run the semantic definition framework on the data.

CATEGORIZE

The linkage processing in the classify step is called as categorizing the data, shown in Figures 6.6 and 6.7, respectively.

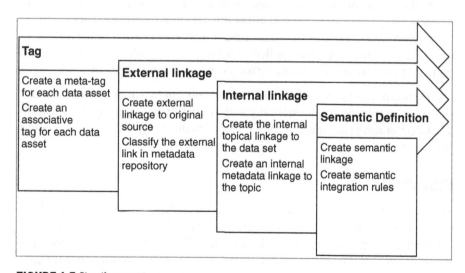

FIGURE 6.5 Classify concept

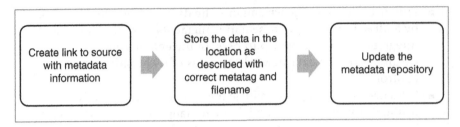

FIGURE 6.6 External categorization concept

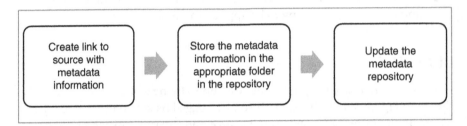

FIGURE 6.7 Internal categorization concept

External categorization is the process of creating a link to the actual data as it was acquired from the source. With this process, the data is linked with metadata rules and categorized into different subjects and dimensions. The external metadata linkage is processed and the actual result is stored in the metadata repository under external categorization.

Internal categorization is the process of linking the data with the appropriate subjects and dimensions that will allow the data to be discovered and used for integration purposes. The metadata rules for this processing is derived from the semantic framework and applied to the data. The result of the processing is updated to the metadata repository under internal categorization.

An important note here is the fact that the data can be categorized under different subjects many times externally and internally. To avoid the complexities of understanding the integration, we recommend using different rule names and subject names.

DISCOVERY

The next step of data accessing involves executing the discovery process, which is the crux of processing social media data into the enterprise. In this step, we execute a series of business rules multiple times on the data set from the semantic processes to create the final outputs for metric execution and integration. The process is captured in Figure 6.8.

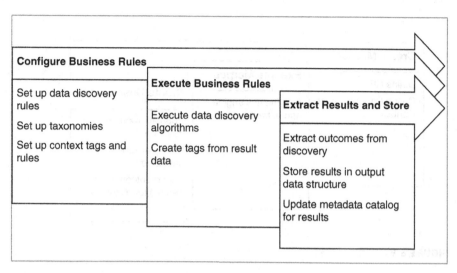

FIGURE 6.8 Discovery process concept

The key steps in the discovery process are the following:

- Configure business rules—The configuration process for business rules is executed in the following steps.
  - Data discovery rules—In this process, we will set up rules for discovering the patterns we want to search and contextualize the discussion or data set from social media. The rules are simple English-like patterns processing on the data set.
  - Taxonomies integration—Once the data discovery process is executed, run a taxonomy engine on the data and create additional semantic layers as feasible. Once the taxonomy is executed, reexecute the data discovery rules for new contexts.
  - Contextualization and tagging—As a final step of processing, create the contextualization setup for the data and tag the appropriate set of contexts and the data applicable to the same.
- Execute business rules—The business rules configured and the data discovery processing and contextualization are executed in this step. The outcomes are stored in the structured database and a file.
- Complete the result processing as the last step. Now the data is ready to execute metrics engine on the top.

METRICIZE

The final step of processing data for access is adding the metrics and key performance indicators (KPIs) on the social media data and integrating the outcomes on analytic platforms and deploying dashboards that utilize new-age

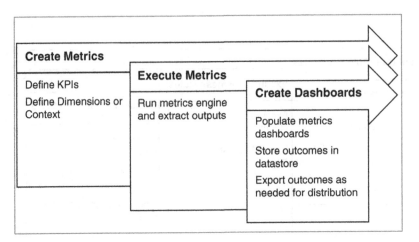

FIGURE 6.9 Metricize concept

BI software for creating powerful mashups that provide enterprise data and social media data in one platform.

The metrics process is shown in Figure 6.9 and consists of three major steps:

- Create dimensions, context, and metrics—The simplest form of metrics for social media data lies in the number of people following a post, number of leaders, influencers, and consumers, the quality of discussion and impact on the brand, the potential action that might be required based on internal analyst and data science team's reviews of the discussions.
- Execute metrics—Create the metrics on an analytic platform and execute them. The outputs from the execution will be accessed for populating the dashboards and also stored for future trend analytics and processes.
- Dashboard creation and execution—The last step is executing the dashboards and exporting the results for further distribution and processing as deemed necessary.

This completes the extraction to accessing processing of social media data. There are several platforms to complete the exercises, and they offer different techniques for the same purpose.

CHALLENGES IN DATA QUALITY

The biggest issue with social media data is the quality of data and the associated context and language of processing the data. While this issue is something that cannot be solved by an enterprise, there are several techniques to improve the quality of data.

- Semantic technology integration—By implementing a semantic framework into the data processing techniques, we can improve the quality of language and sentiment associated with the language.
- External libraries—By implementing external language libraries, we can navigate the hierarchical issues surrounding the data. For example, in social media we might have customers or prospects discussing different levels of product hierarchy, and some of the products may be very old and not even available, or the vendor might have been acquired in a merger situation. The external libraries are useful to solve these types of situations.
- When to stop worrying about data—The rules engines process quality once on the data, we need to stop worrying about the value of data and its quality once this process executes. What you see is what you get at this point.

DELIVERING THE INFRASTRUCTURE

Integrating social media data is a challenge to an enterprise as it involves several rules of processing, involving the integration of taxonomies and semantic framework and adding metrics on the data. There are three basic deployment techniques for processing this data

- On-Premise—Create a solution architecture on-premise and involve the business teams to process the data rules and taxonomy integration. The issue here is how does the integration of the analytics platform happen, who owns the systems versus the data, who is the sponsor, and how is the budget managed.
- On-Cloud—A software as a service option is to deploy the solution on a cloud architecture. The issues that need to be solved are how to create the analytics and dashboard for the enterprise to use and consume.
- Outsourced—A third option is to outsource the entire operations to a third-party company that specializes in the data and create a collaboration suite for data access and usage

DELIVERING ACCESS TO DATA

The access of social media data in the enterprise has a few architectural components that must be designed and configured for a successful implementation.

- Security—The biggest concern that an organization will have is the security of social media data and access to the raw and processed data. A set of security rules needs to be implemented for securing and accessing data both from within and outside the organization. The security rules will need to cover the following

- Data encryption—Any data that is related to a key customer, prospect, or product needs to follow rules of encryption based on customer attributes per login.
- Data masking—Any data that is related to competitive research needs to be masked based on user access criteria
- Data availability—All data will be available for usage based on a user's login.
- Distribution channels—To create a successful social media deployment, users need to get access to data in a timely manner. These distribution channels can be portals, collaboration channels like SharePoint or Drupal, or analytical integration channels like Tableau or R.

HOW DOES THE ENTERPRISE USE THIS DATA

As we conclude the access of data within the enterprise, the most common question that bugs the reader is how does the data get used. There are several important programs in the enterprise that get benefit from integrating social media data

- Competitive research
- Customer sentiments
- Brand status
- Loyalty programs
- User influence and reach

By implementing an appropriate set of analytics to the data as business users access and analyze the data, we can leverage the data for completing these programs.

Key takeaways from the chapter

- Access of data—from a data platform perspective needs, the appropriate semantics and metadata to be associated with the data.
- Security of data—from an internal organization perspective, the data needs to be secured using tagging and classification techniques where the appropriate resources have access to the data at the right time.
- Store once and use many times—Needs to be the concept applied when collecting and storing the data. Adding the right tags and classification is key to achieving the strategy of accomplishment for the data.

The next chapter will focus on integrating social analytics into the enterprise. We will discuss the analytical techniques to process this data beyond discovery and talk about the different programs that can use the data for business success.

Social Platforms

CONTENTS

The world we live today revolves around constant sharing and exchange of news whether it is internal to a family or internal to a country, or just news that is shared between people of communities and countries and conversations that are happening on the subject or revolve around the subject. This type of interaction has changed the universe in terms of connectedness and availability, building communities in minutes, and creating a viral impact on people and behaviors.

In recent times, this type of impact has been provoking the thoughts of enterprise leaders on how to leverage the end state from a within-the-organization perspective, improving collaboration between different teams and geographies, and creating a vibrant virtual organization. The outcome of these moves will be better employee engagement and productivity.

The question is not why to do this type of platform integration and implementation but what are the platforms, what behaviors will these provide internally, and how they will promote the next generation of growth and scalability needed by the enterprise.

UNDERSTANDING THE SOCIAL NETWORK LANDSCAPE

In the distribution and sharing of information and news, there is a wide variety of platforms serving a multitude of needs. Each of these platforms provides their users with a different set of features that enable them to collaborate, share, publish, and post information as deemed useful to their community and context of discussion. From a corporate perspective, each platform produces data and information that can be utilized to create a better view of their brand, business, and services to customers and prospects.

Before we look at the data, we should explore where the data is derived from and how the leading platforms can provide a pool of valuable information ready to be leveraged by enterprise analytic programs.

Blogging Communities

Blogging is a popular form of social media and it creates massive amounts of social data. A blog is a personal website or page that is designed to allow the user to post or create content that is generally presented in chronological order and often engages its readers with the tools to discuss and comment on the content within the blog. Popular communities include Blogger.com, a site hosted and owned by Google; WordPress.com, a pioneer in the blogging space that hosts more than 75,000,000 blogs (Figure 7.1); and Tumblr.com, which hosts more than 146,000,000 blogs. Each of these communities offers its users customizable features and interfaces designed to enhance content sharing and interaction with readers. Topics within these communities are wide ranging, covering everything from automobile maintenance to pet animals. As each blog author creates content, the information becomes available to the public and can be leveraged by companies who have the capacity to ingest the unstructured data. The challenge is to identify blogs and readers that align with the topics important to your business. The authors of these blogs can become a critical part of your social strategy, providing unvarnished insights into your products or services.

Wordpress.blog statistics

- WordPress hosts over 75,000,000 blogs
- 398 million people view 14.3 billion pages each month
- Authors create more than 36 million new posts per month
- Readers create more than 63 million comments each month
- 44% of WordPress blogs are in languages other than English

While these numbers can be a bit overwhelming, it's clear that blogs are popular social media tool and that blogging communities can be a great source of social data. Blog data is often made available via application programming interfaces (APIs) or from authorized data resellers. Distilling the unstructured blog content to useful data is covered in detail in chapter 5.

FIGURE 7.1 Blogging sample. *Source: Wordpress.com Website*

7.1 SOCIAL MEDIA

Social media can be defined as a group of technologies that assist users in sharing and creating content that is consumed via social networks based on Internet applications. This type of media differs from that of traditional sources, as the creators are often not affiliated with traditional news or media outlets. Social media is the tool of citizen journalism and it leverages immediacy and highly defined reach to deliver content to interested consumers.

Crowdsourced Content

May people think of the Internet in terms of technology, but it is actually the people that add the most value to the Internet. The best algorithms and content management systems are incapable of competing with the "Wisdom of Crowds" when it comes to presenting information and identifying trends. This term was popularized in 2004 by author James Surowiecki in his book titled *The Wisdom of Crowds: Why the Many Are Smarter than the Few and How Collective Wisdom Shapes Business, Economies, Societies and Nations*. The case studies and examples in Mr. Surowiecki's book highlighted how leveraging the insight of a group will often outweigh the insight of a few. This model is put to great use on crowdsourced content sites in the social sphere.

Excellent examples of social networking while leveraging and creating crowd-based content are the news aggregation sites Reddit.com and Digg.com. These free-to-utilize social media sites provide a framework where users can write or post content on just about any topic. The community votes the content up or down within its category, effectively curating the thousands of posts so a reader can quickly see what's topical or trending within the topic area.

In the case of crowdsourced content, the users within the community add value to the content by adding comments, debates, and conversations around it providing significant insights into each topic or post. For example, the crowd-sourced community at Reddit.com is extremely large; the site hosts more than 81 million unique monthly visitors. In 2012, the site delivered 37 billion *pageviews*, hosted 260 million comments, and approximately 400 million votes on content. When you explore this community, you can see the conversations about national brands, popular products, and important news trends, all trending in one environment, with context and tags attached to the entire set of discussions (Figure 7.2).

Social media data can provide a lot of insights on competition, prospects, customers and more data. Integrating the highly unstructured information will require significant analysis and data integration techniques to join it to existing systems within your organization. The data is highly valuable but is often anonymous in its origin so the information might be best utilized in an aggregated format to provide a high-level view of these topics from a sentiment standpoint.

FIGURE 7.2 Reddit.com sample. *Source: Reddit.com*

Discussion Forums

Discussion forums are perhaps the earliest form of social media platform. Early adopters of Internet technology may recall news groups or special interest groups (SIGs) that were hosted on the early websites and systems connected to the Internet. These communities were rooted in technical topics but eventually expanded to cover just about any category that could attract an audience. These platforms matured and are now hosted on consumer-oriented social networking sites.

Discussion forums are especially valuable from a social analytic standpoint as they are highly focused in their content and provide a candid view of the topic being discussed. The content is often unstructured in nature but contains various social data types that can be leveraged into better enterprise decision workflows. Flyertalk.com is an excellent example of a discussion-driven community, which hosts discussions centric to the airline industry. Topics include frequent-flyer forums, travel news, luxury hotel discussions, and advice on all things airline related.

Content created within this community can be utilized to identify trends, brand awareness, and sentiment and other valuable content directly focused on the airline and travel industry. Communities like Flyertalk can create vast repositories of data; the site's "Mileage Run Deals" discussion area has 32,000+ discussion threads that contain more than 460,000 individual posts and comments. Each of these posts is written by a community member who is an avid flyer in search of deals and routes that will add to his or her frequent-flyer account, helping him or her to achieve the highest level of airline status. These types of flyers are invaluable to the airline industry, so it makes sense that understanding them better and engaging with them on a topic they find important will add value to the relationship between them and their favorite carrier.

Gaming Communities

Gaming communities are a fast-growing destination on the Internet. They provide a targeted service to users who are seeking online entertainment. While these users are interacting with the games within these communities, they produce an immense amount of behavior data as well as sentiment data. At first blush, it might be difficult to understand what an enterprise company can learn from online gamers. A large portion of these users leverage mobile devices to play, thus sharing location and device data with the host community. Players choose games that they enjoy, and for many these games align with real-world brick and mortar businesses like gambling and entertainment companies. Lastly, many of these online games are friend based, where a player can select real-world friends to play with online. These relationships create data that helps to define the social graph of players. thus giving more valuable social data to companies that leverage the information.

Zynga is a leader in the gaming community sector. They operate some of the Internet's most popular games, including FarmVille 2, which hosts 40 million active users, and Words with Friends, a game similar to Scrabble that serves 12 million players. These games focus on entertainment while the gamification algorithms urge players to include friends and expand their social network. Zynga is a great example of a company that is driven by social data insight. They collect more than 60 billion rows of data and 10 terabytes of semistructured information every day. It's common for Zynga to host more than 600,000 players at a time on its platform. The company's servers generate 13 terabytes of raw log data every day. Not all of this data is socially produced but it's a great example of how Big Data challenges go hand in hand with companies that are serving communities of users on the Internet.

7.2 GAMIFICATION ALGORITHMS

Gamification is the application of game-playing techniques into activities or processes in applications or software. When companies apply gamification to interactions with targeted users, it's generally an attempt to motivate users to take steps within their service or system that align with the company's business goals. Simple examples would be a restaurant review website providing its users with merit badges presented on their profile as they become bigger contributors to the community. Or a geolocation community rewarding its community members with discount offers when they interact with the service, motivating them to make purchases and thus generate revenue for the company. The algorithm aspect of this definition is simply the steps and the code embedded within the applications that deliver the game-playing motivation and effect.

Live Streaming

As the Internet and social networking sites have matured, they have enabled innovative forms of content delivery. Live streaming communities are on the rise and are delivering social media content in real time to the masses, serving the content needs of large popular consumer groups and niche consumers alike. The content varies widely, covering everything from how to quilt to leading-edge tech programming. Much of the content is consumed live, but most communities archive episodes so consumers can watch when it best suits them. This type of time-shifted content consumption puts more control in the consumer's hands and is putting pressure on traditional content companies. Less costly video equipment and Internet bandwidth advancements have enabled this form of socially driven content to prosper and reach an audience greater than many network TV shows.

An added feature of viewing this type of program is the social element. Most programs offer live chats during the episodes and discussion forums to support viewers in an ongoing way. Not all of the content carried by these live streaming networks is citizen created; most of these platforms are partnering with traditional content companies to extend their reach and to help them engage in a more social way with viewers. Ustream is an early pioneer in the space and serves both content consumers and citizen broadcasters. Each month, the platform serves more than 600,000 viewers, who visit more than 1 million times every 30 days.

Ustream is an excellent source for better understanding the viewing habits of a community. The socially engaged user community shares sentiment data, rich media data, and behavioral data, all of which is highly valuable to companies striving to better understand their customers. Another excellent example of Live Streaming communities is Justin.TV, a network of nearly 8000 channels. Entrepreneur Justin Kan, who dedicated himself to lifecasting his entire personal world, founded the site in 2007. Among the site's many channels, consumers can find high-quality cutting edge topic-specific content. A leading channel on the network that often covers news and information centric to enterprise software is Silicon Angle, and their program "The Cube" is anchored by industry experts who analyze and report on technology issues. To date, their content has been viewed nearly 7 million times. In comparison, Fox's hit program Glee was only reaching 7.47 million views in December 2013.

Each of these live streaming platforms generates a deep and valuable set of data on its community as a whole and on individual users. Understanding their areas of interest, viewing habits, and social commentary on the content creates an in-depth insight that traditional lead generation tools or customer relationship management systems cannot produce or leverage. These platforms for social analytics are a goldmine to innovative companies that can tap into this information.

Micro-blogging

Micro-blogging is a social media service designed to broadcast short-form social content. The distribution model is different with micro-blogging sites who provide a simple "Follow" function in their platform, making it easier to consume the content shared on their platform or via a client application.

The leading platform for micro-blogging known worldwide is Twitter (Figure 7.3). Twitter allows users to share 140 character-length messages with a wide audi-

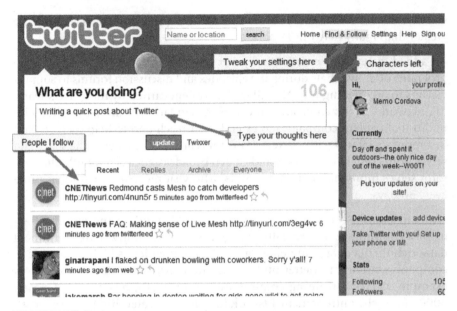

FIGURE 7.3 Twitter home page.

ence in a near-real-time manner. Authors can include web links and photos in the posts that help consumers reach content beyond the original 140-character message. The system also uses a hash tag system to help categorize the subject matter of the post. An example of a Twitter style hash tag would be #SocialA-nalytics. When a post on Twitter includes a hash tag, it becomes highly search-able, providing a filtering tool for someone who is leveraging the Twitter post for social analytics or consumption.

Twitter is one of the most popular sources of social data in the world. The content on the platform is rich with sentiment data, location information, and general information that can help to drive marketing campaigns, customer ser-vice work processes, and more.

Twitter was founded in 2006, and as of late 2013 it served 240 million unique monthly visitors. Twitter makes its data available to the world via a public API that can be accessed at http://apiwiki.twitter.com/. The site provides in depth documentation on how to acquire Twitter data and what that data means. Twitter data can be integrated into enterprise applications and databases by parsing the JSON document provided via the API. The Twitter API is an excel-lent source to experiment and build proof-of-concept projects based on its data. As your needs mature and you require access that exceeds the public API feeds, you will need to engage a licensed reseller of the Twitter social feed. Gnip (www.gnip.com) and DataSift (datasift.com) are two of the leading resellers.

7.3 JSON

JSON, which is an acronym for JavaScript Object Notation, is an open-standard format that uses human-readable text to transmit data objects consisting of attribute–value pairs. It is used primarily to transmit data between a server and web application, as an alternative to XML.

Sharing Networks

Sharing networks present an interesting social opportunity to gain insights into community users. Sharing networks are platforms whose main focus is to enable users to share content; examples would be networks like YouTube, where end users can consume and share video content (Figure 7.4); Flickr, where users share photo content; or LastFM and Pandora, where users consume music and share playlists and sentiment about the music they like.

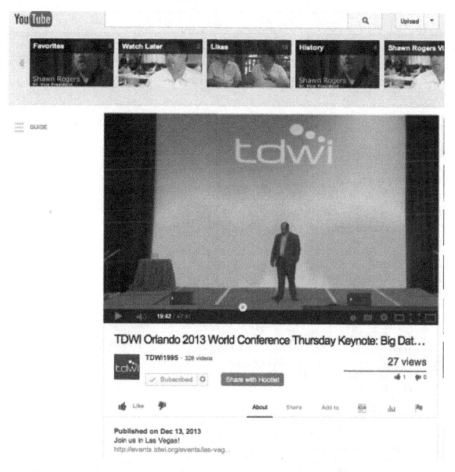

FIGURE 7.4 Krish Krishnan on stage at TDWI World Conference. *Source: TDWI Youtube Channel*

YouTube is the world's second-largest search engine next to Google. The site hosts 1 billion unique users every month. YouTube serves 6 billion hours of video content monthly and uploads 100 hours of new video content every minute. Each video shared on the network contains data that can be harvested for social use. Titles and descriptions point the user to content that fits their interests and in turn allows social experts to match this relationship and leverage it. YouTube's social data content falls into the area of rich media data. The sheer size of the user community and the content make it a social data source that's hard to ignore.

On the surface, rich media data doesn't appear as easy to deal with as perhaps the JSON feed from Twitter, but the public API at YouTube allows social data professionals to harvest data based on keyword searches, comments by video ID, tag search, video uploads by user profile, and favorite videos by users' profile.

```
<entry xmlns="http://www.w3.org/2005/Atom">
    <id>http://gdata.youtube.com/feeds/videos/LoXY8
S4iknE</id>
    <published>2009-01-19T18:57:55.000Z</published>
    <updated>2010-07-21T14:46:17.000Z</updated>
    <title>NicholasKristof favorited a video on You
Tube</title>
    <category term="VideoFavorited" label="Video Fa
vorited"/>
    <link rel="alternate" type="text/html" href="ht
tp://www.youtube.com/watch?v=LoXY8S4iknE&feature=y
outube_gdata"/>
    <source>
        <link rel="self" type="application/atom+xml"
 href="http://gdata.youtube.com/feeds/users/Nichol
asKristof/favorites?max-results=10"/>
        <title>YouTube - Actor - Favorites - Nichola
sKristof</title>
        <updated>2010-07-21T13-40-10Z</updated>
    </source>
    <service:provider xmlns:service="http://activit
ystrea.ms/service-provider">
        <name>YouTube</name>
        <uri>http://www.youtube.com/</uri>
        <icon/>
    </service:provider>
    <activity:verb xmlns:activity="http://activitys
trea.ms/spec/1.0/">http://activitystrea.ms/schema/
1.0/favorite</activity:verb>
    <activity:object xmlns:activity="http://activit
ystrea.ms/spec/1.0/">
        <activity:object-type>http://activitystrea.m
s/schema/1.0/video</activity:object-type>
        <id>object:http://gdata.youtube.com/feeds/vi
deos/LoXY8S4iknE</id>
        <titletype="text">On the Ground with Nichol
as D. Kristof - Win a Trip with Nick</title>
```

```xml
    <content type="text">New York Times columnis
t Nicholas Kristof invites college students to win
 a trip to Africa with him. The winner will report,
 blog and vlog from the field. To apply, upload a
video response here or submit an essay. You can fi
nd all the info at http://www.nytimes.com/onthegro
und</content>
    <link rel="alternate" type="text/html" href=
"http://www.youtube.com/watch?v=LoXY8S4iknE&featur
e=youtube_gdata"/>
    <link xmlns:atommedia1="http://purl.org/synd
ication/atommedia" xmlns="http://www.w3.org/2005/A
tom" rel="enclosure" type="application/x-shockwave
-flash" href="http://www.youtube.com/v/LoXY8S4ikn
E?f=user_favorites&app=youtube_gdata" atommedia1:d
uration="156"/>
    <link xmlns:atommedia1="http://purl.org/synd
ication/atommedia" xmlns="http://www.w3.org/2005/A
tom" rel="preview" href="http://i.ytimg.com/vi/LoX
Y8S4iknE/0.jpg" atommedia1:height="240" atommedia
1:width="320" atommedia1:duration="00:01:18"/>
    <category scheme="http://gdata.youtube.com/s
chemas/2007/categories.cat" term="Shows"/>
    <category scheme="http://gdata.youtube.com/s
chemas/2007/keywords.cat" term="Win a Trip"/>
    <category scheme="http://gdata.youtube.com/s
chemas/2007/keywords.cat" term="Nicholas Kristof"/
>
    <category scheme="http://gdata.youtube.com/s
chemas/2007/keywords.cat" term="Nick Kristof"/>
    <category scheme="http://gdata.youtube.com/s
chemas/2007/keywords.cat" term="YouTube"/>
    <category scheme="http://gdata.youtube.com/s
chemas/2007/keywords.cat" term="Contest"/>
    <category scheme="http://gdata.youtube.com/s
chemas/2007/keywords.cat" term="Africa"/>
    <category scheme="http://gdata.youtube.com/s
chemas/2007/keywords.cat" term="The New York Times
"/>
    <category scheme="http://gdata.youtube.com/s
chemas/2007/keywords.cat" term="NYT"/>
    <category scheme="http://gdata.youtube.com/s
chemas/2007/keywords.cat" term="NYTimes"/>
    <category scheme="http://gdata.youtube.com/s
chemas/2007/keywords.cat" term="College"/>
    <category scheme="http://gdata.youtube.com/s
chemas/2007/keywords.cat" term="Student"/>
  <gnip:statistics xmlns:gnip="http://www.gnip.
com/schemas/2010" favoriteCount="155" viewCount="1
87797"/>
  <gnip:rating xmlns:gnip="http://www.gnip.com
/schemas/2010" average="4.277311" max="5" min="1"
numRaters="238"/>
 </activity:object>
```

```
<author>
    <name>NicholasKristof</name>
    <uri>http://www.youtube.com/user/NicholasKri
stof</uri>
    </author>
    <activity:author xmlns:activity="http://activit
ystrea.ms/spec/1.0/">
        <activity:object-type>http://activitystrea.m
s/schema/1.0/person</activity:object-type>
        <link rel="alternate" type="text/html" lengt
h="0" href="http://www.youtube.com/user/NicholasKr
istof"/>
        <id>http://gdata.youtube.com/feeds/users/nic
holaskristof</id>
    </activity:author>
</entry>
```

The public API at YouTube requires the user to pass variables to the system to invoke the correct system and data response. The code example above requests the data on a video a user has favorited and the payload returns data on the author, topic tags, video URL, title, and more, creating a valuable bundle of data on this users. From this data, social analytic professionals can capture the information and use it to build informed views of clients and their interests.

Special-Interest Platforms

There are hundreds of social networking sites that could fall into this category. Special-interest platforms are social network sites that are highly focused on specific topics instead of wider areas of interest. These sites often deliver similar features and benefits to their users as the bigger, more general-interest sites but while maintaining highly focused content. AllRecipes.com is a special-interest site aimed at people who enjoy cooking and baking. All of the content on the site is recipe oriented and directed at the how-to audience with this interest.

The advantage of a community like allrecipes.com is the way the users interact with the content and their mere presence on the system. Utilizing special-interest sites qualifies the interests of the users. Companies in the cooking and baking industry will see the members of this community as prime prospects for their services, and their presence on the network qualifies them as such. Special interest and highly focused content doesn't necessarily equate to small audience sizes. Allrecipes.com hosts 700 million visitors per year and during peak times like Thanksgiving, the community consumes 7.2 million pages of content per hour. Special-interest social communities are excellent sources to help you better understand your customers and prospects.

Social Platforms

Social platforms like Facebook, LinkedIn, and Google+ are the leaders in the market from an audience perspective and from a social data perspective. These sites make up a huge percentage of the world's online social interactivity and each has APIs and data access options to collect highly valuable and insightful social data.

Ratings and Reviews

Ratings and review communities have become great sources for social sentiment analysis on brands and services worldwide. There are many sites across the Internet that enable consumers to have a voice on topics from restaurants, hotels, retail, and more. Each of these sites help to segment the community so social professionals can clearly identify interests and attitudes of the community and its members. The content model for these sites is a mix of site-supplied infrastructure and content and reviews and tips from its members. One of the leaders in this space is TripAdvisor, a travel community with a wealth of resources that includes travel-reviewed hotels, restaurants, and activities across the globe. TripAdvisor hosts a community of 57 million members worldwide, all of whom have an interest in travel. The community has authored more than 125 million reviews on 3.1 million businesses and properties in 134,000 locations. Members have also contributed 17 million photographs to be shared with the community. TripAdvisor is a good example of a hybrid special interest and rating and review community. Companies in the entertainment and hospitality industry watch this community closely to understand travel trends and monitor brand for positive and negative sentiment.

Based on what we have discussed so far, you can see how the social analytics platform from blogging to shared services collaboration plays an important role in the creation and promotion of the social media and its analytics for your personal and enterprise life. Here is a checklist that we recommend you create and utilize in the social platform establishment for the enterprise.

- Enterprise and external web properties—Does your Web presence tie into your social presence? Does your website promote Twitter, Facebook, and YouTube handles and a fan page? Are there a real-time stream of tweets, Facebook comments and blog links about your company, products and services available on the website?
- Blogs—Does your company have an official blog? Do you share stories with customers and encourage guest blog postings from customers? Do employees have personal blogs in which they discuss company-related topics, including competition and markets? Do you have governance and policies around blogging and do you monitor the same effectively and does it produce efficiency with relationship management between you and your customers and prospects.
- Twitter—Does your company have a Twitter presence and do you have marketing, sales, and research groups participating? Are any employees tweeting company-related content? Does the team measure the number

of followers, the number of tweets produced, the number of tweets that are retweeted, the number of times the organization is mentioned on Twitter, and the customer sentiment ratio of positive to negative mentions? Does the research team compare the contrast between your company and the competition? Does the executive team get dashboards and metrics from Twitter activity delivered and do they participate in Twitter?

- Facebook—Does your company have a Facebook fan page or group? How is it being used? How many members and fans do you have? What are the conversations like on your wall? Is the page being used to drive people to the organization's website to purchase products? If so, what kind of response do you see to promotions on the Facebook wall? How often does a competitor follow your style of Facebook activity and how often do you have price-based competition on this channel?
- Video media sharing—Are there company videos uploaded to YouTube, Google, and any other video-sharing sites? How many views and comments are these videos getting? How often do you upload videos? Do you find videos uploaded by public capture or employees on these sites?
- Media sharing—Are there company pictures uploaded to Flickr, Slideshare, Google+, Picasa, Tumblr, Instagram, Snapchat and any other picture-sharing sites? How many views and comments are these pictures getting? How often do you upload pictures? Do you find pictures uploaded by public capture or employees on these sites?
- Podcasts—Does the company produce podcasts? How many downloads are they getting and who is downloading this data? Where is this information hosted and who manages its lifecycle?
- Crowdsourcing sites (Innocentive.com; Kaggle.com)—Does your company use crowdsourcing sites for solving problems? Are these efforts saving resources? What problems are they solving at what costs?
- Online reputation—Does your company engage in listening and monitoring to when the organization, its products, or its executives are mentioned online? Do you know how many mentions you are getting and on what channels do they happen most often? What is the sentiment ratio for every period of time?
- LinkedIn—Does your company have a LinkedIn page? How many of the company's employees are on LinkedIn? How many of them have more than 100 connections? Do these employees know how to use all of the site's features?

All of these social media platforms have become necessary to compete in the world of business and personal space alike today. If you are dreaming of being an agile and fast-paced company in the next generation, adapting to this platform and learning to utilize its resources are needed to become second nature to the enterprise.

Today people are connecting globally using an array of social software applications. They are joining social communities and sharing their ideas, opinions, sentiment, and much more information using social media. This wide adoption of social software provides the opportunity to create these dynamic communities. The wide acceptance of social software is providing the capabilities to link service across B2B (business to business), B2C (business to consumer), and B2P (business to people) solutions.

The goals for implementing the social media platforms inside the enterprise should have a set of outcomes, some examples are as follows:

- Grow market share across geographies
- Optimize services and costs across marketing, sales, customer services, product research
- Discover and deliver relevant information about your organization and competitors at the right time
- Listen and learn from outside and internal exchanges, questions, and interactions
- Engage and respond to every situation with customers and prospects as part of their community
- Integrated social and marketing information back to your products, services, research, sales, and marketing teams.

How will implementing a social platform strategy help?

- Business to people connections are improved, linking your customers, prospects, partners, and employees
- Fast, fun, and friendly connections link people to the right information to drive commerce.
- Communities formed by members using your products or competing market products or services become your partner network across the value chain.
  - *Improve your digital brand identity management.*
  - *Improve marketing campaign effectiveness with faster feedback and better metrics.*
  - *Grow revenue by linking social interactions to micro-marketing campaigns and ad syndication.*
  - *Build brand loyalty by enabling advocates to easily contribute.*
  - *Gather ideas to drive innovation and research.*
  - *Enhance customer services by listening and responding quickly.*
  - *Focus competitive intelligence.*

Social intelligence provides the integration across all your social software and digital properties:

- Improve governance by applying industry-leading standards of practices.
- Manage content across social sites, micro-sites, and communities.
  - Extend search engines: *Be the "data discovery leader"* that connects people to relevant content.
  - Tap streaming conversations and monitor the patterns with analytics models.
  - Link to affinity groups via micro-marketing campaigns, to your products and promotions.
- How does social networking and communities apply to research and development?
  - Use structured searches to gather social content and feed ideation.
  - Collaborate within an interactive social network with role-based information delivery.
  - Direct ideas to internal experts, researchers, within a secure community.
  - Gather metadata from user surveys, tags, scoring, and enrich text-mining tools capabilities.
  - Enable "food-for-thought" collaborative services to read, tag, score, and route posts to internal experts.
  - Integrate gathering and collaboration with analysis process to share and collaborate on content.

There is tremendous business value in connecting people based on their personal or professional interest. These connections are linked to your web presence across B2B, B2C, B2P, and online properties. Connect your online properties, social sites, marketing events, products, and services and

- Link marketing analytics to social analytics to drive effective micro-marketing campaigns?
- Create affinity based communities within fitness, healthcare, emergency planning, recovery, and child safety
- Connect people within affinity groups to your products, promotions, and social services
- Increase relevance of content delivered to customers across the digital marketplace and within online communities
- Improve the focus of marketing campaigns
- Proactive listening to the voice of the customer and prospects
  - Improving customer service
  - Improving their brand and image
  - Improving the effectiveness of their promotions

Enterprises today are embracing these concepts and creating robust platforms for internal usage and thus efficiently creating collaboration on all aspects from all teams to provide very insightful business impact in terms of growth and employee satisfaction.

The key takeaways from this chapter are the following

- Platforms—There are multiple social media and network platforms that have emerged and grown to be recognized leaders. These platforms and their APIs can be integrated for use by the organization to create and promote an internal employee social media platform.
- Behaviors—The overall outcome for a platform implementation is the change of behavior from an internal organization perspective. The behaviors that will change is the increase of collaboration and transparency between teams in the organization. While companies can use the benefit of knowledge management strategy and exercise in this aspect, the foundational difference to be understood is the fact that we are using data transformations to drive behaviors, and these changes need subtle management and constant collaboration.
- Collaboration—This is a very important aspect of the implementation and needs to be utilized as the constant change in the entire process. The collaboration can be implemented as a process using SharePoint and similar tools within the organization.
- Gamification—Strategies to create a simple process of collaboration, agreement, and liking of content and its importance in the organization and between teams. From the simple like on Facebook to retweets on Twitter, these types of applications of strategies will create the adoption of social media platforms for internal usage in the organization.

Further discussions on these and more interesting concepts, ideation, and tools are in the book in multiple chapters and case studies.

CHAPTER 8

Social Business Intelligence and Collaboration

CONTENTS

Social analytics is the end state result set that arises from social media integration with business intelligence, and this has created a new and exciting form of insights for business users, helping them in understanding the actual movement of the S-curve and assisting in creating blue ocean strategy in the marketplace. How does this kind of integration work and how can enterprises leverage maximum benefit from this data integration? There are two specific areas that benefit the best in any enterprise where one is customer and the other is products and services. These are the two money-spinning or impacting subjects that continue to worry enterprises. This chapter will focus on discussing the integration of social media and business intelligence data areas and the outcomes associated with the analytics and the associated blue ocean capabilities that can be leveraged (Figure 8.1).

INCREASING CUSTOMER FOCUS AND TRANSFORMING TO CUSTOMER-DRIVEN ENTERPRISE

In the past decade, the evolution of social media and its influence on business has been unprecedented. The bottom line message is "The customer is no longer outside the organization, rather the customer is shaping the organization,"

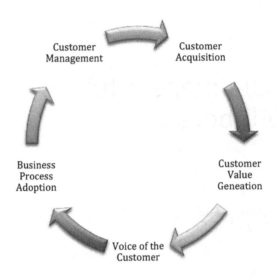

FIGURE 8.1 Customer Connectivity Lifecycle

and if you want to thrive in this grappling economy as a product or service, your approach to evolving the business requires a "customer-centric" approach.

What does customer centric mean? Providing a superior customer experience across an organization's products and services and providing the customer with undisputable value and satisfaction is the simplest form of being customer centric. One can argue that most organizations today adopt this approach, but the reality is there are a handful few who have really embraced the concept and made gains, and there are others who have tried and failed, and yet others who probably have a lip service approach.

Here is the lifecycle approach to customer-centric evolution.

In the picture above, we can see that post–customer acquisition the biggest hurdle to cross is creating a value quotient with the customer. This is a very crucial step, which in the past was accomplished by multichannel marketing with mail, catalog, and coupons. That strategy was great when you had a "product" or "brand"-driven customer strategy. Now the equation has shifted balance to "customer"-driven product and brand creation strategy. This fundamental shift has created the need to treat the customer as a stakeholder in the business. In order to get this approach correct, you have to understand the "new" customer, who is very social media savvy and can be very influential about your products and/or services to a large network or crowd of people.

Before we understand the social media impact and integration, there are a few terms to learn a few important underlying concepts or surrounding themes

- Crowdsourcing—first coined by Jeff Howe in a June 2006 *Wired* magazine article "The Rise of Crowdsourcing"—is a concept where people form communities of shared interest, but the community is formed in the Internet. The basics of the concept revolve around the fact that degrees of separation between individuals have reduced greatly because of the Internet, and this has created a virtual "crowd." We all know since the dawn of time, the crowd has been a powerful force in creating and paving ways for brands and their associated products and services. The new "crowd" based on communities forms a very powerful vehicle that can be tapped by organizations in helping drive the creation of its products and services. The net result of such an endeavor will help foster brand loyalty and increase the market presence from WOMM (word-of-mouth marketing). If you need to see this type of activity in action, see www.ideastorm.com.
- WOMM—Not a new concept, this kind of person-based marketing has existed since ages. Regarding customers before the mass commoditization of telephones and television, there was a marketplace in every community and it had a wide range of products and services. The vendors in this marketplace relied on a loyal set of customers, who in turn did them a favor by bringing in new customers in the form of friends and family. This is what we call today as WOMM. The difference here is the reference and WOMM behavior happens on the Internet and in community forums, shared interest websites, and personal websites such as Facebook, Linkedin, Tumblr, etc. This behavior is a key trend that needs to be measured.
- Long tail—In statistical terms, the long tail is a variation of the normal Pareto or Gaussian distribution, where the larger population of the statistic rests in the tail. The "long tail" was popularized by Chris Anderson in an October 2004 *Wired* magazine article, in which he mentioned Amazon.com and Netflix as examples of businesses applying this strategy.

The long tail strategy is driven by volume of business at lower cost, resulting in higher profits. This model has been since embraced by a number of organizations.

In order to embrace the "new" type of customer, organizations need to understand the three concepts and apply them to their business models. Such an exercise will help establish a business case for creating the program popularly called as "Voice of the Customer." This type of a program will create a sense of stakeholders among the customer base and foster a growth of community around the business, thus enabling the brand to succeed in new markets, in new products and services areas. This model is not something that all organizations can benefit from, but conducting an experiment will always provide a basis for making the determination.

To the benefit of the organizations, there are several technology innovations that have happened in the past five years, including the following: Hadoop and its ecosystem (Mahout, R, PIG, HBase), Cassandra, Google MapReduce, Data Warehouse Appliances (second and third generation), high-speed disk arrays, and in-memory technologies. All these put together in solution architecture will enable the technology platform for social media integration into the organization.

Let us now look at tapping into Social Media and how it will benefit any organization that deals in the service industry.

ACME Inc has decided to implement a program called "Voice of the Customer." This program aims at promoting better understanding of the customer and their sentiments expressed in conversations with the call center representatives across channels, including email, chat, surveys, and phone conversations.

To accomplish this program, ACME Inc has to follow the steps outlined below

1. Establish several contact points or listening posts to hear and understand the customer and their solutions / grievances. The first important step in understanding the customer is to "listen" to the customer.
2. Extract the data from these listening posts, and examine the trends expressed in these conversations
3. Integrate the result set into reporting and analytics engines via data integration
4. Visualize the trends and metrics from the same
5. Provide the data to relevant business users to derive the intelligence and understand the customer intelligence.

Fast-forward to the next step, ACME Inc has implemented a technology solution platform that can provide a rich insight into "Sentiment Analysis." The software can capture speech and convert the same to text and, further, analyze the data within the text to gather the sentiment of the conversation. Post this step, the software will categorize the conversation tone as positive or negative and the associated keywords and trends that led to the inference.

While this is a huge step in connecting to the customer, the unfortunate scenario here is

- The customer sentiment expressed in the conversation is not categorized based on the context. For example, the customer makes the following statement: "I have been very frustrated with a particular service offering and the number of times I had to follow up for the same. I'm not going to engage in the pursuit any further as there is minimal support.

I'm very disappointed." In this situation, the sentiment analysis software will help verify that the sentiment is negative, the reason is minimal support, and the customer is disappointed. What the business user will miss here is the big picture that text mining and analytics will look at—customer is unhappy with certain services as he had to follow up and received minimal support; he is unhappy in this context and wishes to cancel the said service. This big picture is contextual in nature, but there are several soft links here, how many more services the customer holds and might cancel, how many other people in his network this customer might influence, or rather how many more customers have expressed such concerns and canceled services. Unless this gap is addressed, the value from the Voice of the Customer initiative is deemed primitive.

- The second listening post is that customers will follow up the conversation with emails. Example: Customer writes an email

  - from: john.doe@myfreecountry.com

    to: msvcs@Acme Inc,.com

    sub: Customer Services Feedback

    Dear ACME INC, I have been a customer for the last 30 years of your services. While the relationship has had its share of highs and lows, in recent times your customer services team has been performing very poorly. The response times have been lagging, there is a lack of urgency to close questions, the intent is to sell more services and not address issues. While we appreciate the self-service channels you have opened, this direct channel has deteriorated. Should this trend continue, I will be forced to consider other alternatives.

    Sincerely

    John.Doe

In this email, there are several key issues and associated sentiments and comparisons. If the customer had written this email and then in a 30-day time frame followed up a call to let ACME Inc know that he is moving on, there was time to react had the email been parsed and an alert raised on potential attrition.

Why is this important, because if John Doe has 50 friends who hear his story, chances are a loss of all 50 customers or, over a period of time, loss of groups of customers that will lead to revenue loss. Now if John doe were to express this in a Social Media forum, there is brand reputation at stake and more customer attrition.

To increase more actionable insights, ACME Inc should go beyond just Sentiment analytics, to integrate data across multiple channels, including email and social media analytics. Not only will this bring better insights, it will provide the organization with the ability to predict and model customer behavior and be prepared to react better in such situations. Additionally the data and analytics will enable the business user community to better address their knowledge base and learnings, and better aid their customer interactions.

AN INTEGRATED APPROACH

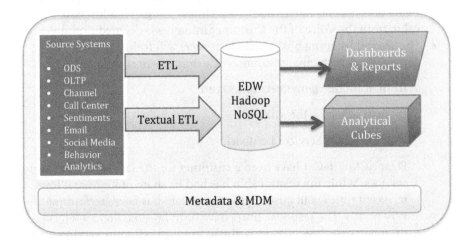

The picture above shows a high-level integration approach where we combine processing structured data from OLTP/ODS systems and process the ETL rules, and alongside process unstructured data from sentiments, email, and social media channels. The advantage of combining the data from both the sources is we can get a holistic view of the customer. The linkage between the different types of data will be enabled by the existing MDM (Master Data Management) and Metadata collections.

ENABLING A BETTER CROSS-SELL AND UP-SELL OPPORTUNITY

ACME Inc has concluded a campaign for a new integrated portfolio services plan to its customers. The campaign has resulted in several calls from the customer community to the call center and business services teams. In this scenario, there is a need for getting real-time access to the customer, campaign, and social media / listening post data. This integrated data set will provide a clear roadmap for additional cross-sell opportunities. Such data can be analyzed and visualized in an all-in-one mashup that can be consumed by the business service executive or call center executive. This will result in better customer experience and drive a true customer-centric approach. The end result will be measured in gains in revenue for the organization.

Example

Caller Customer: Name: John Doe; ID: 123456AZFSCST

Campaign: NMSCSWW-3456XX2011

When the customer calls, the system loads in the information and provides the following data

Customer LTV
Last transaction date
Last product purchased
Last campaign responded to
Customer stickiness
Customer life events
Customer cross-sell opportunity
Customer social media affiliations and presence (as traceable or a generic customer behavior model)

This data when presented to the business services executive or call center executive will form a guiding portal for them to understand the customer, their current situation, the relevance of the call, and answer their questions in a more focused customer centric approach, and provide excellent customer experience. There is further more data that can be extracted from the content management, contracts, and other financial data that can help provide an enriched customer experience.

BUSINESS BENEFITS

The business benefits from the integration exercise include the following

- 360-degree view of the customer
- Revenue leakage identification and recovery
- Cross-sell and up-sell opportunities
- Better customer connect

The power of integrating social media data will enable the evolution of a customer-centric approach to build business brands. Better connect to the customer enables a better wallet share and creates a sense of importance to the customer. From the discussion so far, we can see the benefits of the next generation of business intelligence and analytics that combines the social media and business intelligence platforms into a single integrated system of insights and solution spotlights. Many large and small enterprises have successfully integrated social media, social software, business intelligence, and analytics into a solution architecture that has reaped rewards in multiple segments, including brand management, solution spotlight, customer loyalty, and last but not the least market share and monies.

The next section of this chapter focuses on the integration and collaboration of social media, social software, and business intelligence platforms, resulting in powerful analytics and mashups.

SOCIAL MEDIA AND SOFTWARE

In the industry today, we can link data and perspectives from customers, services, competition and products across call center, B2B (business to business), B2C (business to consumer), B2P (business to people), C2C (consumer to consumer). Internet forums, portals, and mobile devices with the features and functional capabilities of an integrated social software solution, and a business intelligence and analytics solution stack will provide a holistic set of insights and analytics enabling and empowering better outcomes. For example, think about recommendation engines from Amazon and how it influenced the course of interpreting behavior analytics in the online industry across advertising, competitive research, customer behavior, product analytics, and discussions across forums and customer-driven websites. The new combination of social media and analytics is providing new generations of applications that enable enterprises to organize, market, and distribute their products and services.

SOCIAL INTELLIGENCE

Social intelligence can be defined as the practice of connecting social media and Internet behavior of human and machines with internal business intelligence and analytics platforms to create collaborative decision support and insights outcomes. The collaborative outcomes from a social intelligence platform can be used to:

- Build and manage brand and image in the market utilizing strategies from personalization and gamification along with analytical techniques from crowdsourcing initiatives.
- Listen and learn from
  - Social buzz monitoring
  - Marketing intelligence
  - Competitive intelligence

- Integrate:
  - Digital media across the enterprise
  - Social customer relationship management (CRM) and community owned and driven processes
  - Marketing analytics with social analytics to target advertisements
  - Web metrics and analytics to drive micro-targeted marketing
  - Gamification analytics and reporting to create a holistic view across affinity groups and market segments
  - Focused content syndication and advertisement management to promote products and services
- Engage with customers and prospects at the right times with the right messages and strategies
- Provide appropriate response to blogs, news, forums, and within communities across social media

How will implementing a social intelligence strategy help? That is a question which is being asked, answered, and discovered by many enterprises. The advantages of a collaboration platform can be useful in the following situations:

- Improved and secure B2B connections within collaborative workspaces, creating synergies and benefits to both sides of an equation.
- Increased success and market presence in online and ecommerce business models, where social media and networks become a primary channel of the business presence
- Smart applications that can be leveraged across multiple-channel customer-centric transformation effort to
  - *Target and improve digital brand identity management*
  - *Increased marketing campaign effectiveness with speedier feedback and optimal metrics*
  - *Targeted revenue growth by linking social interactions to micro-marketing campaigns and advertisement syndication*
  - *Gamification-driven approach to build brand loyalty by enabling advocates to easily contribute their likes and recommendations*
  - *Driving collaboration and inviting the customer to drive innovation and research*
  - *Enhance customer-oriented transformation success by listening and interacting quickly*
  - *Empower an effective competitive intelligence strategy*

Apart from the business-oriented benefits, social business intelligence provides the integration of data to drive highly effective analytics across all your digital properties.

How do we apply social media data, data warehouse data, and communities to research and development, competitive analytics, and more?

- Use structured searches to gather social content and feed ideation
- Collaborate within an interactive social network with role-based information delivery
- Direct ideas to internal experts, and researchers, within a secure community
- Gather metadata from user surveys, tags, and scoring and enrich text-mining tools capabilities
- Enable "food-for-thought" collaborative services to read, tag, score, and route posts to internal experts
- Integrate gathering and collaboration with analysis process to share and report content

SOLUTION ARCHITECTURE

The collaboration of social analytics and business intelligence needs a two-step process of understanding. There are segments of data that we are discussing here are external data and internal data. The external data has certain characteristics that we need to understand, the most relevant ones are listed here and this list will grow and change

- Formats can be varied
- Semantics may or may not exist for all data
- Language can vary for data
- Velocity of data generation can be varied
- Data is ambiguous
- Data complexity needs to be managed
- Ownership of data sources need to be managed
- Data quality needs management
- Data interpretation needs management
- Analytics cannot be assigned across the entire set of data
- Geospatial encoding of data is not feasible across the entire set of data
- Video data needs to be managed as speech and images to derive clarity and assign meaning
- Picture data needs to be managed as image and needs intervention to create a lineage and derive clarity

To manage all these processes for external data, it can be tedious and sometimes the effort can be a waste of time if the analytics do not pan out as anticipated. Remember the issue here is no user requirement or integration requirement is applicable until the data is ready for analysis and integration. In order to manage the external data integration into the ecosystem, we can use the process shown in Figure 8.2.

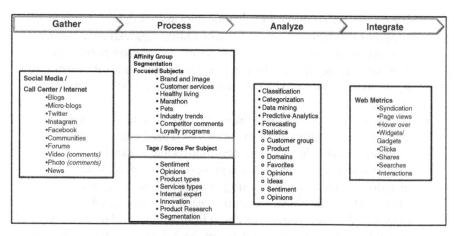

FIGURE 8.2 External data integration process

The external data integration process is a series of steps that needs to be planned and implemented by the enterprise that is interested in an integrated social analytics solution for the enterprise. There are four distinct processes that need to be completed for this process, and to ensure if these steps have been implemented appropriately

- Gather—This is a process to collect data from the following sources
  - Social media / call center / Internet
    - Blogs
    - Micro-blogs
    - Twitter
    - Instagram
    - Facebook
    - Communities
    - Forums
    - Video *(comments)*
    - Photo *(comments)*
    - News

  How does one gather data from so many sources, formats, semantics, languages, distributions, and more? This is where we bring in the concept of "listening posts," which are set up to crawl and listen for specific patterns of data for collection. Listening posts can be set up at different points of data generation and sharing. Some of this data can be purchased from companies like Nielsen and GNIP.
- Process—The data gathered from sources needs to be processed for internal integration and consumption in decision support and analytics. In this stage, the typical actions include searching for patterns

of data, extracting the contexts of the data and its usage, identifying the impact of the data, the sentiment and adding tags, extract keywords, semantic relationships, and segmentation, integration points. The most interesting aspect of this step is the creation of attributes and the segmentation of data, which forms the foundation for analytics and integration stages.

- Analyze—The most interesting stage of analysis of the data happens in this step. The output from the prior step is used with analytics from traditional models like SAS and new models like R, Mahout, and other analytical engines. The data as it is processed through these layers of analytics provides some interesting insights and we can capture the outcomes from these analytics into repeatable model-based analysis with larger and different types of data both from volume and data perspectives. One of the most successful analytics in the industry today is the sentiment analytics from consumers, and it has created both a segment of specialists and a set of companies that do this type of analytics.

- Integrate—The last step of the process is to create an integration foundation with semantic and metadata-driven integration becoming the key point of focus. In this stage, the data is already processed, quality issues addressed, contextualized, and ready for metadata-driven integration with data from structured systems. The output of this step is a series of files with the appropriate metadata and semantic data available along with the result sets.

A note here is the ability to introduce the data auditability process for the external data. This is achieved with the integration of an audit, balance, and control system that is already present in the enterprise but extended to add the different data management and processing steps.

The processing of internal data for the analytical and mashup steps is simpler than the external data. The data is extracted from the system of record and brought over for integration. This is explained in Figure 8.3.

The conceptual solution architecture and the associated systems that are integrated and deployed for social intelligence and analytics in the organization are shown in Figure 8.3. As we can see from this concept, the listening posts form the source systems for raw unstructured data that is collected by the enterprise. The data is derived into a landing zone as files using a ETL like process. There are different systems that will be applied here, including streaming databases, stream of files, raw data as collected from the Internet, and more. A typical system that will be used by many organizations is a text analysis engine that can be used to process the unstructured data with English-like rules. If we are focused on sentiment analytics, we will use a sentiment analytics engine at this stage. Technically, the infrastructure for this layer can be completely in

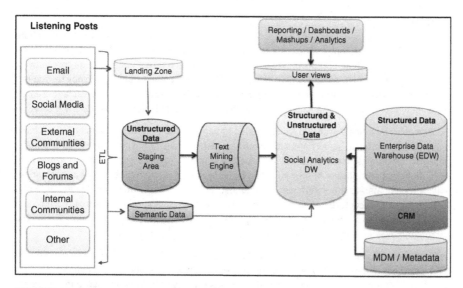

FIGURE 8.3 Solution architecture concept

Hadoop or NoSQL systems, as we will be working on files, and the distributed data-processing capabilities of these platforms lend a great deal of support to process large amounts of data at the same time. There are several implementations of this concept in the industry, and some of the leading companies have got IP on their approach (hence we cannot discuss the same here).

Once the data is analyzed, it is loaded to the social analytics data warehouse where the internal data from data warehouse, MDM and metadata, CRM, and other systems are integrated and the output is provided to business analytics and research users for further analysis and decision support usage. Some enterprises take this data and distribute it to vendors and partners using SharePoint or Drupal systems.

In summary, as we have discussed in this chapter, the integration and collaboration between the data and its producers and consumers creates a lot more insights for the enterprise, and the decision support analytics that can be implemented based on these insights provide a lot more prediction and statistical analytics capabilities.

CASE STUDY: OPTIMIZING HOMEPAGE WITH INTERNAL DATABASE TO INCREASE GROWTH AND EFFICIENCY

Challenge

To drive measurable business results by developing an integrated digital marketing program that incorporates search and affiliate channels to maximize the effectiveness of one of the world's leading logistics company's marketing budget. Optimize their homepage to improve conversion rates.

Solution

A fully integrated channel strategy was developed to ensure that pay-per-click (PPC) and affiliate activity worked in harmony to maximize the effectiveness of digital campaigns. Maximized cost-effective PPC by pushing brand campaigns and top-performing terms to provide the core activity, alongside further generic and tactical campaigns to increase visibility. Continual copy testing encouraged click-through rates, and daily optimization and time targeting reduced wastage. Search messaging was applied to reengage users who had not converted in order to encourage sale.

Built an effective affiliate program with a small number of key volume-driving affiliates. Continual optimization of affiliate activity and testing of new technologies to further improve conversions. Implementation of a tiered commission structure to deliver guaranteed return on investment (ROI). Constant recruitment of new affiliates, incentives, and voucher codes drove performance-solidifying affiliates as a key performance channel. Utilized PPC affiliates—implementation of a PPC affiliates to recapture lost sales via direct competitors bidding on their terms. Formulated space and ensured a constant presence in positions 1–3 for all key brand terms. Result—150 percent increase in month-on-month revenues from affiliate channel.

PPC optimization was achieved via testing of new search features such as ad rotation optimized for higher conversions, automated rules for strategic key words, as well as ad site links. We have also launched a mobile campaign to further increase the overall brand exposure in the digital space. Conversion optimization was chosen to further boost the performance of the paid search campaign. We first performed a conversion and usability audit, highlighting areas of the landing page that could be optimized toward conversion. A series of A/B and multivariate tests were then rolled out over a 5-month duration, increasing performance significantly. Integrated reporting dashboard not only provided detailed analysis by channel but also provided a platform to generate further.

Result

- Exceeded revenue target by >80 percent
- Strongest performance year-to-date
- Year-on-year (YOY) growth on all conversion rates
- YOY revenue increase following optimized multi-channel strategy

Social Media and Network Monitoring

CONTENTS

Social media can be defined as a collection of content created by people using accessible publishing technologies, thereby creating information in formats that are varied and drives user participation and potential drivers and insights into how people discover, read, and share news, information, and content, simply transforming monologues into conversations and democratizing information, transforming people from content readers into publishers. The first eight chapters of this book dealt with different aspects of the ecosystem and platform for social media, including case studies from vendors and participants. This chapter will focus on going beyond just monitoring social media and its associated networking. We will look at the associated networking, legal issues, and compliance issues in the world of social media, how companies need to evaluate these issues and go from where they are to the next levels of social media integration within their organizations.

A "shiny toy syndrome" is the name that many enterprises have called their social media exercises. While the opportunity to engage with customers, prospects, competition, and the whole world is available through the social media space and its associated tools, there is always a pressure that builds with the strategy and its execution in the enterprise. Are we doing this right? Is this the right strategy and will this result in us getting the answers we need? All of these questions can be answered only as the strategy and its execution are conducted. This means integrating the use of agile cycles of execution as mistakes need to be corrected on identification and occurrence. The following are the key steps that need to be watched when implementing a social media platform:

- Learn the ropes of social media and the focus areas that your organization needs to glean from. The key information from social media can be the impacts from customer, product, or competition and prospect areas of the enterprise. Focus on what you need from the data. This is step one from a monitoring and information perspective.
- Crawl before you walk in the monitoring of social media and the associated networks. The crawl step is the most important key in creating a base platform as it involves the interpretation of data with human intelligence. Yes, from creating the crawlers for data collection to integrating the data, you need to understand each step of the process, unless you show this patience and pursuit you cannot win in the long run in this initiative.
- Each community is different in your users and participants within the social media circle, and these are the communities that are formed out of interest in the products or services that you as a company offer. And the participants of these communities provide you insights into both you and the competition. What we learn is these communities often do not involve you in a direct or sponsor fashion and your participation is welcome as a participant. Get help from these communities by identifying the topics of interest and the leaders from the different boards. Encourage them to participate in your surveys and sponsor events, where you can get these communities to come in-person and participate. These efforts are not to persuade them to buy only your products or services, or talk positive about you, but to understand the users what they consider as best or better efforts from you as a company. Often these communities also create a powerful online presence and provide a global voice; for example, the Avon Walk For Breast Cancer, which started as a small effort and today runs across 29 cities as a 2-day event with millions of dollars collected as fundraising.
- What to learn from these communities in the social media and Internet is the million-dollar question that crosses your minds as organizations. What do you monitor and how do you react? How do you respond to queries and questions? What information is deemed competitive and useful to establish markets in new regions and acquire new customers in established markets? Some of the key monitoring and networking opportunities include the following:
  - How users interact in any community is the first monitor that needs to be established. This will create the viewpoint of understanding the users and what they feel about the market in terms of services and products. Apart from the user sentiment, the most important features to look for and monitor are
    - Leaders across the board on different topics and issues
    - Influencers and influential users across the topics

- Geographic and economic behaviors
- Economic and demographic behaviors
- Just participating in these activities alone will not suffice for monitoring the network. While you get the insights, you need to participate with transparency, which needs to be established and built in your user community. Read related blogs: global and local perspectives are needed and will be extremely helpful in monitoring the situations and provide you with help to participate with transparency.
- The golden rules to become successful are the following
  - "Be transparent"—It doesn't mean sharing what you had for lunch
  - Disclose conflicts of interest, make your intentions known

BRINGING THE EXTERNAL TO THE INTERNAL – HOW TO CREATE A PLATFORM

For organizations engaging in creating a platform for implementing social media internally, the key points are categorized as follows

- Goals—A clear and transparent set of goals needs to be added as the primary drivers for the effort and the benefits that will be aligned to both the employees and the company. The goal statement should be explanatory and inviting, not demanding and exploratory. This step is needed both from a top–down and bottom–up perspective to start the innovation approach for the next generation of the enterprise and employees. One of the questions that always need to be answered is why a social media–like platform? Can we not exist with knowledge management platforms? Be clear to explain the fundamental goals of the exercise and outcomes.
- Outcomes—They are considered the definition of success for any program in the modern world. In implementing social media–like platforms, the key outcomes expected are
  - Collaboration between employees and teams
  - Better understanding of context related to internal research and external data from Internet and other sources
  - A collective dashboard of problem and solution options applicable to different realms
- Platforms—Regarded as technical solution architecture, they need to be clearly understood by all business users within the organization. The key here is to promote collaboration and joint ownership of solutions as applicable to the problem whether internal to the company regarding branding or campaign or a situation that needs customer advocacy and call center management. The platforms have to be well integrated from the backend data collection and integration, discovery process,

tagging, classification, extraction, contextualization, categorization, and structured output for integration with analytical platforms for model execution, and finally ready for visualization and integration.

- Analytics—The most important concept that will provide the correct outcomes is the analytics associated with all applications of the data integration and monitoring. This requires governance and stewardship as different teams for different reasons can contextualize data and analyze outcomes. The analytics from this initiative need to be classified as internal data and implemented as a separate cluster of information from a governance perspective.

- Governance—To create a successful program in the organization, governance needs to be implemented both from a technology and a data perspective. The reason for this aspect to be considered repeatedly arises from the complexity of the exercise, and any misstep will result in troubles for the entire enterprise from both user adoption and participation and delivering successful outcomes. Governance has been an Achilles' heel for many organizations engaged in business intelligence and data warehousing today and should not be the case in this type of platform development and implementation.

- Visualization—The visualization of data will be implemented with new technologies like Tableau, Qlikview, and Spotfire. The primary reason for this approach is the mashup capability that is offered by these technologies to marry data from different systems using metadata(business) and providing opportunities to inspect and visualize data from the perspective of an event and how the reaction of the enterprise was to the event. This type of visualization needs a few pieces of metadata to be created apart from the business and technical metadata. The additional data is the source system, the date of the original event, and the internal systems that touched the data and users. Based on the visualization requirements and the key performance indicators (KPIs), the additional metadata will provide the integration rules with keys to evaluate for discovery and analysis.

- Monitoring—An important key aspect is internal monitoring of data and users collaboration. There are multiple needs for this analysis based on the fact that data from external sources is loaded for discovery and then we implement analysis and tagging on the same. The requirement to monitor the users arises from the fact that the same data are extracted by different users and explored for their context of usage, which will need clarity of explanation and usage of other data to create any outcomes.

These are the key concepts to focus when creating the platform for the enterprise. Let us understand the outcomes-based approach from a monitoring and legal compliance perspective.

Situation: A leading cookie manufacturer is interested in launching a new series of flavors that will open more market opportunities. The marketing team creates a campaign on social media platforms including Twitter and Facebook to promote the new flavors and the concept. In examining the reaction of the market, the team is stunned to see major criticism of the product and how new flavors can be harmful to the public. Added to the rants are images of the production factories with pollution and dusty conditions that are even more bizarre as they do not match any location of the manufacturer. The questions begin to pile up from the board and executive teams on how these issues are coming together and who is creating the negative campaigns. The legal team advises the executives to release a statement about the entire situation and their investigation, while advising the internal sales support and competitive research teams to start monitoring internal and external data traffic and network usage specifically with the brand name.

Data: The data gathered from monitoring external traffic is a mixed collection of the company brand and images and videos. The data comes with metadata about the users, domains, IP addresses, and dates of creation and posting of content, content statistics, and more. This metadata is needed to be captured for analysis and examining the underlying trends and user attitudes.

Analysis: The data was executed with a taxonomy-driven discovery platform to tag sentiments, especially negative and rant-related type of data. This discovery helped create the separation of good and bad data from multiple terabytes. Once the data was classified, a detailed analysis revealed the following facts:

- There were multiple regions that were posting comments on the cookie manufacturer
- There were comments and data that did not belong to the manufacturer but were associated due to misspelled tags
- There were artifacts of the company that were posted by former employees who had stolen the data and artifacts
- There are geographic and demographic attributes that did not align with the manufacturer or the products at all but were tagged and posted by some users who had access to the handles of the manufacturer on social media networks.

Outcomes: Based on the analysis of the data and the findings discovered, the legal teams advised the following:

- The manufacturer needed to close all the handles and change passwords across the social media sites.
- The first set of information that was posted after the password changed was to clarify the findings

- The next set of actions was to follow up with legal action on the different users and domains that posted wrong information.

PERSPECTIVE ON SOCIAL MEDIA TOOLS

Social media campaigns on social networks need to be able to track any mention of the brand, be it good or bad, categorize it, and reply to it in real time. And do it for multiple brands, day in and day out, on a budget and with hard metrics to live up to. They use uberVU extensively and in the recent media magazines have spoken about the reasons of using the platform and what goals it has helped them achieve. In discussing the usage of the platform with the teams, here is a perspective:

- What are the reasons for using uberVU?
  - I looked at the other social media buzz–monitoring tools and used a few in my previous work, so I already had experience with them. But obviously the price ranges are massively different. The entire high-end ones are terribly expensive. The product and output you get from uberVU is just as good as the more expensive options out there. Plus, you get the reports, sentiments, graphs, and all the pretty things.
- How does it make your life better?
  - I know that it's constantly tracking every bit of activity. It just works very well. It's very user-friendly. Easy to get on with like when somebody new comes on I don't need to spend too much time training or explaining to them what needs to be done. They also have online support, which is fantastic. It's just a brilliant service.
- Why is it important to constantly track what's going on?
  - We are living in a real-time world right now and uberVU allows us to document and to keep track of any activity. This is good for our clients, as it shows the value we are bringing. It shows that we've had impact on buzzes, messages, and views. Without showing our value, we do not have a company. uberVU helps us a lot to show our value to our clients.
- What's wrong with just using Twitter search?
  - We need to be able to document and check what's happened in the past. With uberVU, you can go back on certain dates to see what's happened. It's been indexed. With twitter, it's not as manageable. It's instant, which is okay. But for what we do we need to be able to go back to a specific date to see what happened on that day, what messages went out and what impact they had.
- If you did not use uberVU what would you be using?
  - Not sure. Sentiment Metrics is far too expensive. Radian6 is far too expensive. What would happen is that we would have to add the cost

on top of our fees in order to use those services. But it would make our service more expensive.

- What is your favorite feature within uberVU?
  - My favorite thing right now is how you manage to calculate the potential views a message has had. It shows how many people might have been exposed to a particular message at a particular time. That's my new favorite thing as it allows me to show clients and say, look, this is the potential.
- Finally, what tips can you give to our readers starting out in social media?
  - Be transparent and realize it takes about 3 to 4 months to build a worthwhile community. Nothing happens overnight. You need to work at it. Create and give away good content. In social media, you have to be open, loving, honest, and transparent. If you're not, it can turn against you.

As we conclude the chapter, we have discussed the social media and network monitoring with a case study and perspective on a software tool that is used in the process. The next chapter will provide the overview on the first project of an organization and its outcomes.

Your First Project

CONTENTS

BACKGROUND

ABC International has been marketing a new product to the market for over 10 months, and the overall results of the new brand and its financial impact have not been very satisfactory. The overall competitive research shows that the product has been received as being expensive and it has loyal buyers in the segment of customers who have a lot of money, but overall the market is being addressed for the requirement by competition, who are not advertising or marketing but relying on word-of-mouth sales across retailers, online channels, and big box network stores. The CMO and his team of marketers have been worried at the overall picture of the brand and engaged a consulting company to advise them as to where the biggest areas of weakness in their strategy and execution lie. The challenges faced by retailers in the industry are seen in Figure 10.1.

The marketing team is convinced about some aspect of the market that has caused a poor performance is terms of sales of a very useful range of products, but are not able to collaborate with the competitive research team to ideate on where the gap lies. There are several data aspects that are pointing to lowering of customer loyalty and attrition of customers, but losing on price or promotion was not an issue that needed to be analyzed. Where is the gap? Why is

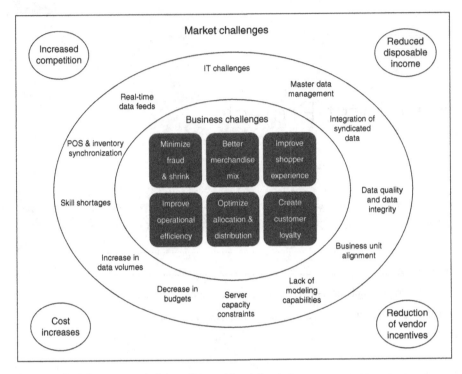

FIGURE 10.1 Current state challenges: Pre–social analytics strategy

customer attrition and acquisition happening at the same time? Who is the prime competition and what is their message?

Additionally the team is convinced that they are not getting all the data needed to integrate the picture, which would help them immensely as it would provide a start-to-finish picture of the entire situation.

SOCIAL ANALYTICS STRATEGY

The consulting company (a leading strategy and research advisory firm) engages in the project. After hearing the fundamental situation and the desired outcomes, the company starts with an assessment of social media data integration and analytics in the enterprise. The goal of the project is to assess, identify, and score the enterprise and its alignment on social media data, focusing on the following areas

- Web business strategy
  - How does the company treat the Internet as a channel?
  - Where does it engage with customers and prospects?

- Who defines the basic approach and strategy?
- How does campaign management work on the Internet?
- Who creates and defines the Web2.0 business model?
- Who defines the measurement strategy of the success on the Web2.0 strategy?
- What data is collected from the Internet?
- Where is the data stored—pre- and postanalysis?
- Who identifies the persona of the customer and prospect on the Internet?
- How does the company interact with customers and prospects on the Internet?
- Pricing
  - What is the pricing strategy?
  - Who determines the price?
  - What is the profit margin?
  - How does the company manage distribution and inventory?
  - Is there a channel-based pricing strategy?
  - What is the average cost per channel of sale?
- Price elasticity and bandwidth
  - Who is the competition?
  - What is the base price of each competitive brand?
  - How many sales advertisements does each competitor execute per day, week, and month, quarter, year?
  - What is the cost of the competitor product for each advertisement?
  - Who is giving the competitive product "free" or at "zero cost"?
  - What analytics and research has been done on price elasticity?
  - Who determines the bandwidth of pricing for the product? Is this different by the market of sale?
- Channels
  - Who were the channels of sale?
  - What is the inventory management strategy for each channel of sale?
  - What is the cost and price management for each channel of sale?
- Partnerships
  - Who are the business partners to the company?
  - What is the supply chain management for the company?
  - Who manages the inventory for the company?
  - How is vendor partnership managed for inbound and outbound vendors?
  - What is the payment strategy for the vendors?
  - Who manages the pricing strategy for the products and how is the payment made to the sellers?
  - How is the online pricing managed?

- How much of competitive research data is integrated into the pricing engine?
- Who manages all the data external to the company from within the company?
- What governance is applied to the data as it transcends through the processes within and outside the company?
- Who manages customer-generated data within the company?
- How relevant is social media data and presence to the employees?
- Marketing
  - How much of marketing as a function is done traditionally and using the web media?
  - What is the budget for marketing within each area?
  - How is the success factor established for each marketing campaign?
  - Who decides the content for the campaign?
  - How many customers and prospects are utilized for each campaign?
  - How many waves are executed per campaign?
  - How many of the campaigns are executed across social media?
  - How do customers engage across social media for campaigns?
  - Who are the most influential customers across social media?
  - How many influencers does it take to convert a prospect?
  - What is the total number of conversions per campaign?
  - How many attritions occur per campaign and how many occur per wave of the campaign?
- Competitive research
  - What research is done about competitive organizations and products?
  - Who leads the research teams?
  - Who owns the research teams?
  - What collaboration exists between different research teams and analysts?
  - How often is competitive data gathered versus purchased?
  - Who governs the data for competitive research?
  - What insights are extracted from this data set and who uses them?
- Customer relationship
  - What are the channels of customer contact and management?
  - How often do you connect with customers?
  - Are your customers loyal? How do you measure this?
  - Are your customers social media savvy?
  - Are your customers brand ambassadors that generate prospects for you?
  - How do customers participate in purchasing products or services?
  - What are the most trusted channels of engagement by a customer?

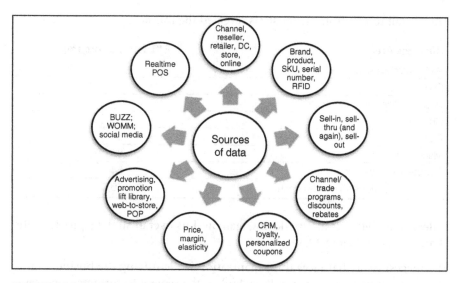

FIGURE 10.2 Data is growing

The fundamental reason for these areas of focus and the questioning can be seen from Figure 10.2.

There has been a rapid increase in the sources of data. In the past, the organization was seeing data from traditional sources like transactional, campaign, and sales systems. Now there are more contributors including customers, social media, online advertising, microtargeted campaigns, price-oriented marketing, and competitive research from a customer perspective. Based on the initial few weeks spent on the research and question/answer sessions, the consulting team came back with the following observations:

- The teams both in collection and analysis are ignoring a lot of data.
- Several competitors are gaining inputs on their campaigns and microtargeting their markets in the same time frame.
- Price models of the products are not matching the competitive space in the market.
- There is no price elasticity strategy and the data collected for this purpose is contributing to 30% of the market.
- The channels of engagement with the customer are all in motion but not producing results as desired.
- The microtargeting exercises are not generated at the correct time, missing the customers and prospects.
- The web business model is a generation old in terms of infrastructure, management, and data strategy.
- Competitive research is not integrating data from social media and Internet sources. This is a very big mistake and needs correction.

The overall results from the analysis revealed the following

Business Area	Efficiency Score (%)
Web business strategy	45
Pricing	67
Price elasticity and bandwidth	71
Channels	65
Partnerships	67
Marketing	83
Competitive research	54
Customer relationship management	76

A deeper analytics of the marketing team and its overall strategy provided the chart as seen in Figure 10.3.

The biggest issue that faces this organization is identifying the business value of understanding its customer. If we look at the score effectiveness in percentage, the issue of understanding its customer is below 50% in terms of its web business strategy. Even if the organization is able to understand and identify the pricing bandwidth and elasticity, its effectiveness in price wars is only 71%, and overall the competitive research effectiveness is 54%. How can we change

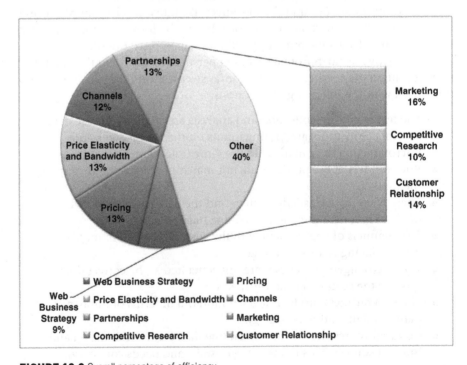

FIGURE 10.3 Overall percentage of efficiency

the game effectively, efficiently, and create a winning strategy? This question became the biggest worry for both the internal team and the consulting team.

Understanding one's customer is very critical, and there are several firms that focus on gathering the data from all external sources and analyze them. These companies sell the data to purchasers for purposes including research. The real business value from social media is derived when you integrate the data and metrics into an analytics engine and can provide insights into

- Revenue leakage identification and recovery
- Improving cross-sell and up-sell opportunities
- Reducing buyer or prospect risks
- Improving consumer experience
- Identifying and classifying affinity clusters to buying influences
- Identifying lost opportunities (price elasticity wars)
- Reputation management

In the market today, firms such as Nielsen, agencies that specialize in aggregating metrics, such as Gnip, Datasift, and Infochimps; and data and metrics providers such as Visible Technologies and Salesforce.com can harness and collect the data.

The overall results of the analysis and the recommended next steps included the following:

- Implement a real-time data collection strategy for all data needed about
  - Customers
  - Prospects
  - Markets
  - Competition
  - Marketing
  - Pricing
  - Sales
- Implement a collaboration suite that will assist the entire team including marketing, sales, and competitive research to look at the data and participate in a gamification approach to decision-making processes, increasing the overall efficiency and effectiveness for the teams.
- Implement a listening platform to listen to web and social media conversations.
- Implement a taxonomy- and ontology-based semantic framework to integrate the data across the different systems.
- Establish a reporting and dashboard platform based on self-service and mashup platforms.

Real-time data is not a challenge anymore to collect, but the sources of data from both inbound and outbound perspective present a set of challenges that

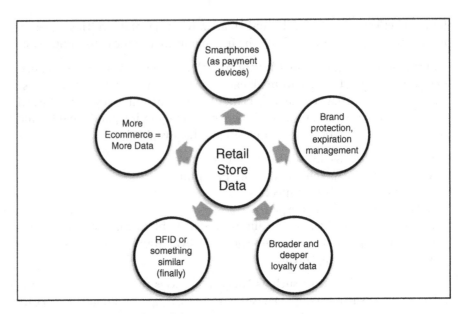

FIGURE 10.4 Data is becoming real-time

need to be addressed. Figure 10.4 shows the retail store data expansion and the targeted footprints that need to be tapped by ABC Marketing and Sales teams.

The deeper outcome that needs to be realized and understood by ABC International is the transformation they need to undergo from being a product-positioned company to a customer-driven company. This transformation will be done at multiple levels in terms of data, analytics, segmentation, clustering, and pricing. Figure 10.5 shows the new alignment (the original picture design and implementation was by Ken Martin, Krish Krishnan, Peter Geovanes, and Shankar Radhakrishnan). In the new approach to customer-driven transformation, we can create and implement multiple solutions for each segment of customers for same or different markets for more than one product and price.

THE FIRST PROJECT IMPLEMENTATION

ABC International took the inputs and outcomes from the research and applied a strategic approach to transform to a customer-driven organization, a tough call but needed immediate attention considering the market and opportunity. Figure 10.6 shows the customer strategy and the areas of focus, which included

- Developing analytical tools and capabilities
- Increasing the breadth and depth of the customer relationship management (CRM) strategy
- Developing exceptional customer experience.

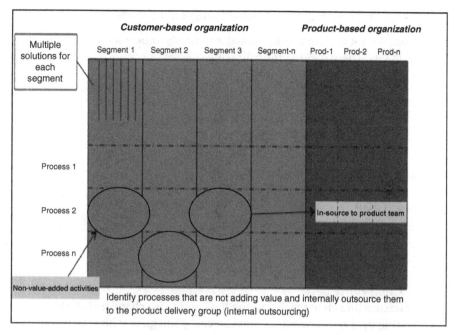

FIGURE 10.5 Customer-centric transformation

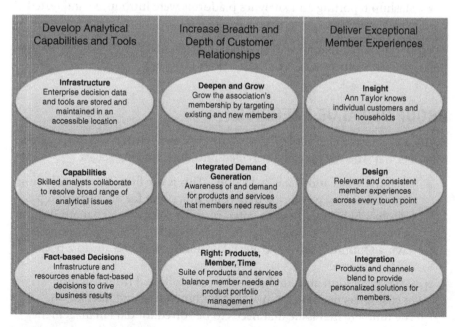

FIGURE 10.6 Customer strategy

The strategy areas needed the following changes to be made

- Data—A lot of data was identified and needs to be added to the current data sets. These include the following
  - Social Media Sites
    - Twitter
    - Facebook
    - Instagram
    - Flickr
    - YouTube
  - Social media data feeds
    - Nielsen
    - GNIP
    - Salesforce.com
    - CoreMetrics
  - Internet forums
  - Customer managed web sites
  - Competitive data
- Infrastructure changes due to the data and these changes included setting up a new ecosystem that can easily integrate with the current state architecture and data strategy.
- Semantic frameworks were needed to be commissioned and included in the overall system.
- Mashup reporting and analytics platforms were introduced and tested for the program.

To ensure that the program was agile and implementable with success, the first step was to implement a proof of value (POV) concept.

PROOF OF VALUE EXERCISE

Figure 10.7 shows the overall picture of the POV exercise that was done by ABC International. The system can be divided into the following stages

- Listening Posts and Data Collection—This is the first stage of collecting data. A listening post is the data collection point for understanding customer behavior. It can be interactive like a survey or chat application or be secluded to monitoring clickstream activity from the customer or having Omniture services collect data and send the results to a back-office platform.
- Data Integration and Analysis—The data collected from listening to customers needs to be managed for processing and integration. The fundamental issue that needs to be solved for data management is the transformation of the unstructured, semistructured, and

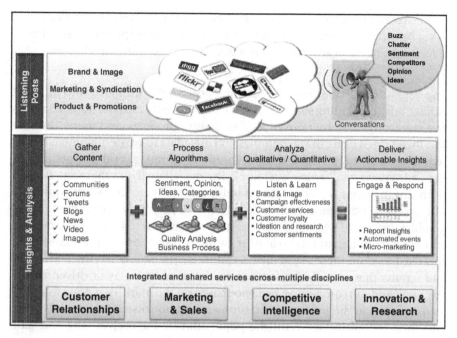

FIGURE 10.7 Proof of value exercise

multiformat data to a structured format that can be easily integrated into the data warehouse and analytics platform. Analysis of this data will require the use of taxonomies and ontologies integrated with semantic framework-oriented design and implementation.

- Analytics—The overall benefit of integrating social analytics will be received by the entire organization on delivery of successful analytics from the data exercises and also in the integrated analytical platform with the data warehouse. The analytics need to be driven off the raw data from the lowest level to the most taxonomy-driven hierarchy structure to understand the multifaceted behavior of the customer across the different stages of the interactions. This would drive the next stage of maturity for the organization to move from product- to customer-oriented transformation.

- Dashboard and Reporting—All the data and analytics cannot be delivered without a strong dashboard and reporting platform. For this exercise, the recommendation was to try Tableau or Spotfire, as the mashup platform in these two technologies allowed data to be integrated based on semantic frameworks seamlessly in the presentation.

- Integration with Data Warehouse—The data from social media needs to be integrated with the data in the data warehouse to create the overall impact from the enterprise perspective. This integration can be completed successfully with a metadata-driven approach using the taxonomy and semantic frameworks for transforming the data into an easily usable asset.

The data was collected from the listening posts and assimilated into different storage posts, including surveys, clickstream data, web conversations, competitive marketing, customer-driven web analysis of products, and more. The data was then tagged using the taxonomies and metadata to create alignment to current state customers, noncustomers, locations, products, and competitors, in the end state to analyze the outcomes. The overall analytics that were derived from this included key performance indicators (KPIs) to discuss the influence of customers, noncustomers, the location of their presence including demographics and social analytics, the products and the interests based on location and demographics, and the behavior of the competition from a market perspective based on these social media and Internet discussions. The dashboard and reports that were driven focused on the product behavior driven by the customer and the competitive behavior based on the markets; reports were created to focus on the influence of customers and noncustomers on each other and their overall influence on the population by themselves. The end-state reports created a trend series and time series analysis of customers, products, and markets based on social media and data warehouse data.

The POV exercise provided the organization with a new set of analytics and market behaviors, which provided them the keys to unlock

- Market behaviors and positioning of products in the market
- Customer behaviors
- Customer financial analytics
- Customer influencer analytics
- Customer follower analytics
- Competition behaviors to markets
- Campaign effectiveness with social media analytics
- Campaign-related behaviors with social media analytics
- Promotion of return on investment (ROI) analytics

These critical areas provided answers to the company on how to align with the market and create loyalty that could be sustained. In addition to the behaviors, it also provided the marketing team inputs on how to create and align the social media strategy for the company, how to create and manage customer-driven and gamified analytics, and how to manage product promotion and campaign in the next generation of customers.

Once the POV was completed, the organization immediately launched a new platform exercise to integrate and manage social media data as an organization

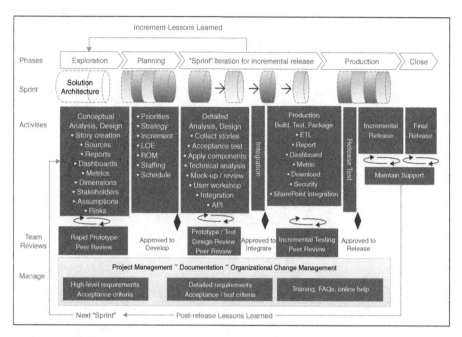

FIGURE 10.8 Solution approach

exercise. Figure 10.8 shows the solution approach that eventually was implemented as an agile platform with incremental ROI and benefits associated with the program. In 12 months from the time the POV was implemented, ABC international had managed to create a new presence in the market and steadily managed to climb the ladder of customer loyalty and had integrated the customers and noncustomers in its innovation journey.

As we come to the end of this chapter, we would like to remind you our readers that social analytics is now in the enterprise and needs this kind of strategy and approach to get it integrated to achieve success. Do not set up a "boil the ocean" approach, as you will never reach an end state. We recommend a small POV approach followed by the agile implementation of the different stages with KPIs and analytics integrated into the end-state solution.

Appendix

SUMMARY

Midwest Financial Trust is a well-respected financial institution with a long, distinguished history. The company has relied on and benefited from a decades-long tradition of word-of-mouth marketing; indeed, referral is primarily responsible for its widely held reputation as a premier provider of financial and wealth management services.

Their reputation in the digital space, however, remains far less developed, and are oftentimes at the mercy of the global web community. As unflattering, often disparaging, content about financial institutions began to surface and propagate on social sites like YouTube, Midwest Financial Trust engaged a leading marketing company that focused on social media platforms (Social Logic) to design an interactive web experience that would not only promote their story in the online space but counter the proliferation of negative press via a stable of sharable video clips.

The power of *sharing* would be critical in building an interactive space that delivered on referral success in the offline world. Also, because the effort would not be supported by traditional marketing, the experience would benefit from having social functionality built in.

SOLUTION

The consulting and internal teams constructed five creative frameworks, each adhering to the strict brand guidelines, in exploring a variety of approaches to presenting a virtual library of video content. Functionality across concepts varied as well, including a YouTube-style sort-by-tag video library, send-to-a-friend links, and a highly customizable clip-building module that enabled users to create their own Midwest Financial Trust presentations for sharing with key stakeholders. Content could also be organized by topic, and optimized for search with relevant tag words.

Beyond offering an in-depth look at the firm's expertise in the financial arena, the content library also promoted a positive online dialogue in communities across the web.

RESULTS

Compelling social proof in the form of first-person video was strongly recommended to combat much of the negative noise, showing real Midwest Financial Trust clients and employees discussing their personal experiences and giving the company's word-of-mouth marketing a much-needed digital voice. This innovative creative solution currently remains with the Midwest Financial Trust team as they consider final production and implementation.

SUMMARY

As one of the United Kingdom's leading banks, BFC Bank is continuously engaged in attracting, retaining, and developing customers. The bank's competitive edge comes from the way its people personally identify and satisfy the needs of potential and existing customers. BFC Bank had been telephoning customers to understand levels of satisfaction, but was conscious that this provided a limited picture of the customer experience, that would not help in increasing the internal focus and understanding of the customer space.

SOLUTION

To create the best techniques to solve this problem, the internal team with some strategy consulting expertise, developed a mystery shopper program that measures the customer journey of a BFC Bank account holder. This involves mystery shoppers opening an account and conducting "real" transactions. Shoppers are selected to match the customer profile, making them credible. A comprehensive feasibility study was conducted to ensure the suitability of the methodology and systems prior to national launch in 2007.

Fieldwork reflects branch characteristics, as larger branches are visited more frequently. Competitor branches are also included for benchmarking purposes. Each branch receives a report on the entire visit and includes first impressions; queue time and handling; inquiry handling; establishing customer needs; product knowledge and recommendations; closing the inquiry and overall experience.

The program is designed to focus on the behaviors of branch staff to identify how they interact with customers while delivering the necessary process. Both behaviors and processes are comprehensively reported and we present clear findings supported by detailed verbatim comments. Branches receive regular performance updates presented in graphical form for ease of understanding. These are linked to a suite of communication and training also provided by the solution suite.

RESULT

The results have been very positive, with the program providing simple-to-use, actionable management information. Throughout 2008, BFC Bank witnessed month-on-month improvement in its mystery shopping scores, as staff became increasingly aware of the importance of providing consistently great service through positive behaviors. These increases are mirrored by BFC Bank's own data that show levels of customer satisfaction on the rise across the country.

In July 2008, the bottom-line results were measured with BFC Bank service against six of its key competitors. Based on basic service elements, overall satisfaction, and propensity to recommend the brand, BFC Bank *"outperformed"* all of its rivals and claimed the best service in the area in 42 percent of its branches.

SUMMARY

One of the world's largest beverage companies needed to find a way of levering a celebrity endorsement to gain cut-through in a tough market. The brand was looking for a technique of messaging that would gain real attention, connecting to the right people and in the right way. The peer referral power of viral marketing offers this promise, but in most cases proves elusive for fast moving consumer goods firms. However, a short video starring a football star proved compelling enough for millions of people to want to send this on. It's the kind of connection all viral marketing sets out to make but rarely delivers.

BACKGROUND

The beverage company needed to find a way of levering a celebrity endorsement to gain cut-through in a tough market. The brand was looking for a technique of messaging that would gain real attention, connecting to the right people and in the right way. The peer referral power of viral marketing offers this promise, but in most cases proves elusive for fast-moving consumer goods firms. The goal desired is the kind of connection all viral marketing sets out to make but rarely delivers.

OBJECTIVES

There was a broad range of objectives behind the campaign.

- Boost brand image
- Boost message association around a sporting event, ahead of the campaign
- Achieve cut-through to a target consumer that had increasingly tuned out from classic media

Given the nature of the medium and the model, it's likely there were additional objectives around the testing and evaluation of new channels within digital marketing.

WHAT THEY DID

Written and devised by a major marketing and social media firm, a short film was created to pre-launch the company's main World Cup Campaign. The campaign included massive television activity and heavy integration between channels, but at its heart was a simple idea everyone can relate to: playing about with a football and keeping it up in the air.

This was the theme used in the viral video placed on YouTube. The style of the video is reportage of a behind-the-scenes filming of a more formal promotional film shoot.

HOW THEY DID IT

It was released two weeks before the tournament began. As the first game of the cup kicked off, it had already been seen by over several million people. Later it was featured in the *Sun*, both in print and online, and it was picked up by ITV and broadcast during their flagship, prime-time program in 2006 to an audience of more than two million people.

The campaign fever spread globally through numerous blogs, social networks, and chat rooms. Consumers were happy to engage, and the messaging was accelerated by the background talk about the World Cup in all media channels. This created the right environment for the spread of the message.

The film has been shared online on video websites and on mobile phones, and fans have been seen trying to emulate the football star's remarkable moves.

EVALUATION APPROACH

Viral video clips can be measured in quantitative ways that track the number of impacts, reach, and in some case frequency. However, in social media spaces like YouTube, the volume of comments can also be tracked, and the language explored for brand affinity measures. More proactive measures of market research can track the brand effect, by asking consumers who are exposed to the viral key brand image questions and then comparing their answers to a control group.

RESULTS

More than 8 million people saw the video clip that began online and was boosted with a small television exposure. The discussions around the video and the campaign spread fast and generated a buzz and discussion that was harder to track but clearly powerful for the brand.

INTEGRATION

The pre-release of viral video content helped amplify the effectiveness of the television campaign. It laid strong foundations for the waves of marketing that would follow and created genuine offline discussion.

As the relationship between viral media and more traditional campaigns evolves, new ways are being discovered to let one feed the other. The edgy reportage feel and the way it was released created a sense that the viewer was in on a secret; YouTube gave the perfect way to share that secret with their friends.

SUMMARY

Objective: Drive sales and consideration for a new car, and build a brand community.

Solution: Run a Facebook ad campaign to launch the brand to the "social generation" followed by sustaining media on Facebook to grow awareness and familiarity for the brand.

Key Lessons: Facebook ads can be a useful tool for driving awareness of a new brand. Nurturing your Facebook community can turn your fans into brand advocates and can drive word of mouth. Cross-media campaigns that are built to be social can be more effective than those that add.

CHALLENGE

A major South Asian automotive manufacturer became active on Facebook when they launched a new urban passenger vehicle in 2009. The vehicle was intended to be a transformational car for the brand and was designed to appeal to Gen Y, or the "social generation." The company saw Facebook as an ideal channel to support the launch of this important vehicle because of the target audience's desire to consume information in social environments. "Facebook has become a natural cornerstone of any social media engagement," says the manager of customer relationship management (CRM) and Digital Marketing at the company. "What we like most about Facebook is that we not only have the opportunity to create a community but we can also engage in targeted advertising." They sought to leverage Facebook's scale, targeting and engagement to create awareness and consideration for the new vehicle. It also wanted to generate familiarity with the vehicle to make people aware of its unique and fresh styling, great value and high level of technology. The company also wanted to build a community around the new vehicle brand and identify influencers who could help spread positive word of mouth about the vehicle among their friends and colleagues.

SOLUTION

Creating familiarity with the Gen Y target audience was a primary goal for the company, in addition to providing the brand with an opportunity to showcase its new line of vehicles and encourage consumer interaction and education about the vehicle's unique features. They were able to create an experience within its Facebook Page where it could showcase stunning visual representations of its products.

In addition to engaging consumers with its products, the company built a custom tab with an augmented reality game called "Go Hamster Go!" The game was highlighted in their creative ad, and its use of face tracking added to the cool factor of the campaign. The company leveraged the natural activities of people on Facebook by using Premium Poll Ads as the primary way to educate its consumers about key product information. For example, in one Poll Ad, they asked the question "What's your favorite setting for your speakers?" as a way to familiarize people with the variety of pulsating light settings incorporated into the vehicle's audio system. "This target expects marketers to come to them with a solid understanding of who they are and deliver customized messaging that is highly relevant," said the CRM Manager. "If our target is the social generation and we're not engaging with them in a social manner, we are by definition not legitimate in their eyes." In order to generate and sustain awareness and consideration, they executed a launch campaign in 2009 and a follow-up effort in 2010. The launch phase consisted of Engagement Ads including Premium Video Ads, Premium Like Ads, and Premium Poll Ads. The company used a mix of Age and Likes and Interests Targeting to reach its customers. After establishing a community with the launch campaign, they leveraged those connections in its sustain program by targeting its fans and their friends. The company's Facebook activity has enabled the company to formulate a unique approach among auto advertisers who typically restrict their media spending to a 12-month period for new-vehicle launches and rely heavily on TV advertising. According to the leadership, their Facebook strategy "is about outreach and building a community—and ideally, one is a function of the other."

RESULTS

The sustained campaign led to a 13-point increase in awareness for the new vehicle, according to a study conducted by media research firm The Nielsen Company.

- According to Nielsen, 14 percent of individuals said their perception of the brand improved after seeing the ad (a significant increase over the control group).
- The Premium Video Like Ads, including the names of friends who had already connected to the company via "Friends of Connections" targeting, resulted in the highest engagement rate for the campaign.
- There are now more than 89,000 people who are part of the Facebook community, which means the brand can reach more than 31 million friends of those fans with Friends of Connections targeting.

The success of launch effort led them to conduct additional campaigns for both the new vehicle and several other models. "Our 13-point lift in awareness is significant and indicates that we've found something that works and we will continue to leverage that," says the CRM Manager. "To have a brand lift like that, something substantial has to happen. We were fortunate that the catalyst in this case was a great product." Their campaigns were also successful in building an engaged and active community around the new vehicle brand. That community has given the manufacturer an additional benefit: the ability to educate consumers about the new vehicle brand and product in a deeper way, which has been critical given the relative youth factor of both the company and vehicle brands. "Our Facebook activity has helped increase awareness of the company. But Facebook has also driven familiarity so that people are not just aware that we exist, but actually are familiar with who we are today." said the CRM team.

THE FUTURE

In the future, the relationship between the company and Facebook is emerging as a partnership: "We have a community that we've invested in and have established within Facebook. We certainly hope to grow that community and to keep it fresh and engaged, with the ultimate goal of encouraging that community to be our friends and our brand advocates." The company is in the process of introducing its product team to the opportunities social media can offer in terms of product development and customer feedback. "We are definitely increasing our investment in social media and you can't really have a social campaign without Facebook," they say.

Since its first foray on Facebook with the new vehicle launch, they continue to conduct innovative and successful campaigns on Facebook across its growing portfolio of cars. Throughout these experiences, "successful social media requires great strategy that's executed with diligence and perseverance in a consistent manner over time—having engagements that add value to the community is what's critical."

The company is also focusing its efforts to create more tightly integrated cross-media campaigns that are built to be social. "The real win is having the different pieces work together as a whole and understanding that each piece serves a different purpose." "It's an evolution for any brand that's been heavy in traditional—the first step is to make a TV ad and then wrap social and mobile around it, but that's not the right way to do it. I tell our creative agency to plan as if they are not even going to be allowed to use TV to get them thinking creatively about building integrated campaigns."

Index

L

Lead generation tools, 81
Legal contracts, 39
Leverage, 75
    Facebook's scale, 133
    machine data, 6
    technologies, 21, 74
LinkedIn, 17
Listening platform, implementation
        of, 121
    social media conversations, 121
    web conversations, 121
Listening posts, 53, 96, 103
Long tail business strategy, 95, 96

M

Machine learning algorithms, 1, 65
Machine-learning model, 52
MapReduce programming model, 66
Market behavior, 126
Market challenges, 116
    pre–social analytics strategy, 116
Marketing, 115, 118, 120
    analytics, 101
    budget, 105
    intelligence, 3, 101
    strategy, 29–30
    team, 115
MDM, 98
Metadata, 34, 36, 57, 69, 98, 102,
        105, 111
    to create alignment, 126
    integration, 35, 60, 104
    repository, 70
Metricize concept
    process major steps, 72
        create dimensions, context, and
            metrics, 72
        dashboard creation and
            execution, 72
        execute metrics, 72
Metrics aggregating firms, 121
Metrics providing firms, 121
Micro-blogging, 81
    social media service, 81
    twitter, 82
        hash tag system, 82
        Java script object notation
            (JSON) document, 82
        marketing campaigns, 82
Microtargeting, 101, 119
Midwest Financial Trust, 129
    power of sharing, 129

production and
        implementation, 130
    reputation in the digital
        space, 129
    solution, 129–130
MongoDB, 66
Multichannel marketing, 95

N

Natural language processing
        (NLP), 4
Network sharing platforms, 83
    Flickr, 83
    LastFM, 83
    Pandora, 83
    YouTube, 83
News sharing, 75
Next best offer, 49
NLP engines, 5
No-SQL database systems, 66

O

OLTP/ODS systems, 98
Online communities, 17
Organizations, 2
    chart and details, 14
    governance, 19
    leverage data, 39
    POV exercise, 126
    project implementation, 122–124
    social data analytics strategy, 3
    technology innovations, 96
    website to purchase
        products, 88

P

Partnerships, business, 117–118, 120
Pay-per-click (PPC), 106
Picture data, 102
Platform analytic functions, 5
    brand affinity, 6
    demographic analysis, 6
    geospatial analysis, 5
    influence analysis, 5
    machine data analysis, 6
    sentiment analysis, 5
    text analytics, 6–7
Platform functions, 4
    areas, 5
Platform implementation, 91
    behavioral change, 91
    collaboration, 91
        sharepoint, 91

knowledge management
        strategy, 91
Point-of-sale data, 39
Portal-based business, 26
Portfolio services plan, 99
POV. See Proof of value (POV)
PPC. See Pay-per-click (PPC)
PPC optimization, 106
Pricing, 117, 120
    bandwidth, 117, 120
    elasticity, 117, 120
    models, 119
Product
    data, 8
    positioning in market, 126
    promotion, 126
Proof of value (POV), 124, 125
    analytics, 125
    dashboard, 125
    data analysis, 124
    data collection, 124
    data integration, 124
    data integration with data
        warehouse, 125
    listening posts, 124
    reporting, 125
Public relations teams, 8

R

Real-time data, 121, 122
    collection strategy, implementation
        of, 121
Refinement, of data, 68
    enhance, 69
    filter, 68
    finalize, 69
    steps in the process, 68
    validate, 69
Reporting platform, 121
Reputation management, 121
Research and competitive analysis
        data, 38
Return on experience (ROE), 20
Return on investment (ROI), 37,
        43, 106
    analytics, 126
Revenue leakage identification,
        99, 121
Revenue leakage recovery, 121
Revenue loss, 42
ROE. See Return on experience
        (ROE)
ROI. See Return on investment (ROI)

S

Sales force automation (SFA), 38
Score effectiveness, 120
Semantics, 102
"Sentiment Analysis" software, 9
Sentiment analytics, 96, 98, 104
Share content, 13
Sharepoint-driven collaboration, 2
Shiny toy syndrome, 107
SIGs. *See* Special interest groups
    (SIGs)
Six Sigma organization, 17
Social analytics, 93, 101, 102
    data warehouse, 105
    ecosystem, 24
    and its adoption within the
        enterprise, 15
    prospective, 15–16
    solution, 103
    strategy. *See* Social analytics
        strategy
Social analytics platform sharing, 87
    crowdsourcing sites, use of, 88
        innocentive.com, 88
        kaggle.com, 88
    enterprise web properties, 87
    guest blog postings, 87
    online reputation monitoring, 88
    podcasts management, 88
    video media sharing, 88
Social analytics strategy, 116
    channels of sale, 117
    competitive research, 118, 120
    customer relationship, 118, 120
    data analytics, social media, 116
    data integration, social
        media, 116
    marketing, 118, 120
    partnerships, business, c, 117, 118
    price bandwidth, 117, 120
    price elasticity, 117, 120
    pricing, 117, 120
    web business strategy,
        116–117, 120
Social business intelligence, 27, 101
    foundational components provide
        data creating, 27
        business intelligence, 30–32
        CRM, 29
        marketing strategy, 29–30
        social media, 28
Social buzz monitoring, 101
Social content, 81, 102

Social customer relationship
    management. *See* Customer
    relationship management
    (CRM)
Social data, 4, 12, 36, 76
Social data types, 47
    behavioral data, 48–51
    location/geographic data, 56–57
    rich media data, 57–60
    sentiment data, 51–53
    social graph data, 53–55
Social enterprise, 11, 15, 16
Social intelligence, 90
    affinity groups linkage, 90
    analytics models monitoring, 90
    brand building and
        management, 100
    competitive intelligence, 101
    data discovery leader, 90
    data integration. *See* Data
        integration
    marketing intelligence, 101
    social buzz monitoring, 101
Social media, 26, 28, 76, 100,
    103, 107
    and analytics, core
        characteristics, 25
        community-driven, 25
        emotion over content, 26
        interactive, 25
        relationships, 26
        user-based, 25
    customer-centric approach, 93, 94
    data integration, 93, 100
    definition of, 77, 107
    implementation, 107, 109
        analytics, 110
            data integration, 110
            data monitoring, 110
        customer impact, 108
        goals setting, 109
        governance application, 110
        internal monitoring of
            data, 110
        outcomes expectation, 109
            context search, 109
            team collaboration, 109
        product impact, 108
    integration program, 64
    listening post, 63
    monitoring. *See* Social media
        monitoring
    platforms. *See* Social media
        platforms

sites, strenth and business, 28
tools, 112
    perspective of, 112
    radian6 technology, 112
    sentiment metrics, 112
    uberVU technology, 112
Social media monitoring, 108
    blogs, 109
    to business goals, 41
    data interpretation, 108
    economic behaviors, 109
    geographic behaviors, 109
    influential users and influencers,
        108
    leaders on the board, 108
    terms of service understanding, 108
Social media platforms, 1, 2, 79, 126
    discussion forums, 79
        flyertalk.com, 79
        frequent-flyer forums, 79
        social data types, 79
        trend identification, 79
    gaming communities, 79
        behaviour data, 79
        mobile devices, use for, 79
        sentiment data, 79
        zynga, 80
    goal outcomes, 89
        market share growth, 89
        outside exchanges learning, 89
        relevant information delivery, 89
        services optimization, 89
        social marketing information
            integration, 89
    implementation, 107
        customer impact, 108
        product impact, 108
    live streaming communities, 80
        Justin.TV, 81
        real time content delivery, 80
        silicon angle, 81
        social element, 81
        Ustream user community, 81
Social media presence, creating and
    engaging, 39
    decide on collaboration, 41
    engage! don't just post, 40
    examine analytics for insights, 41
    make a plan and content
        calendar, 40
    monitor what works best and does
        not work, 40
    post your content with
        consistence, 40

Printed in the United States
By Bookmasters